Andrew Hammond

English
for Common Entrance

Durston House School
12 Castlebar Road
Ealing, London
W5 2DR

Hodder Murray

A MEMBER OF THE HODDER HEADLINE GROUP

Acknowledgements

The Publishers would like to thank the following for permission to reproduce copyright material:

Photo credits
© Andrew Holt/Alamy, p.7; © Bettmann/Corbis, p.11; © Peter Schouten/National Geographic Society/Reuters/Corbis, p.15; Ken Biggs/Stone/Getty Images, p.19; © Morton Beebe/Corbis, pp.23, 143; New Line/Saul Zaentz/Wing Nut/The Kobal Collection, pp.27, 112; © Tim Graham/Alamy, p.36; Homer Sykes/Alamy, p.40; S.T. Yiap/Alamy, p.44; Steve Bloom Images/Alamy, p.48; pierre d'alancaisez/Alamy, p.52; Mary Evans Picture Library/Alamy, pp.56, 83, 115; Roger Hutchings/Alamy, p.60; © Pictorial Press Ltd/Alamy, p.69; Photofusion Picture Library/Alamy, p.74; Edward Parker/Alamy, p.78; BananaStock/Alamy, p.87; © PCL/Alamy, pp.91, 120; Andrew Fox/Alamy, p.152

Acknowledgements
© BBC Books, p.7; © Thornton Butterworth, p.11; © The Independent, p.15; © Kuoni Travel, p.19; © Newsquest Media Group 2005, p.23; © Nev Pierce, p.27; © Faber and Faber, pp.31, 32, 40; © JM Dent, p.36; © Bloodaxe Books, pp.52, 60; © Hodder Children's Books, pp.74, 78–79; © Doubleday, p.83; © Theresa Breslin, p.83; © Viking, p.87
Except from YOU DON'T KNOW ME by David Klasso Copyright© 2001by David Klasso

Reprinted by permission of Farras, Straus and Giroux, LLC

The publishers would like to thank Christopher Ellott for his help with developing this manuscript.

Although every effort has been made to ensure that website addresses are correct at time of going to press, Hodder Murray cannot be held responsible for the content of any website mentioned in this book. It is sometimes possible to find a relocated web page by typing in the address of the home page for a website in the URL window of your browser.

Hodder Headline's policy is to use papers that are natural, renewable and recyclable products and made from wood grown in sustainable forests. The logging and manufacturing processes are expected to conform to the environmental regulations of the country of origin.

Orders: please contact Bookpoint Ltd, 130 Milton Park, Abingdon, Oxon OX14 4SB. Telephone: (44) 01235 827720. Fax: (44) 01235 400454. Lines are open 9.00–5.00, Monday to Saturday, with a 24-hour message answering service. Visit our website at www.hoddereducation.co.uk

© Andrew Hammond and Christopher Ellott 2007
First published in 2007 by
Hodder Murray, an imprint of Hodder Education,
an Hachette Livre UK company
338 Euston Road
London NW1 3BH

Impression number   5 4 3 2
Year   2010 2009 2008 2007

Cover photo © D. Robert & Lorri Franz/Corbis
Typeset in 11 on 15pt Franklin Gothic Book by Phoenix Photosetting, Lordswood, Chatham, Kent
Printed in Italy

A catalogue record for this title is available from the British Library

ISBN: 978 0340 90789 4

Contents

PART ONE
Unit 1 Non-fiction

Paper 1:
Section A: Non-fiction

Unit 2 Poetry

Paper 1:
Section B: Poetry

PART TWO
Unit 4 Essays

Paper 2:
Section A: Studied Literature

The English Common Entrance Examinations

The Common Entrance Examinations are produced by the Independent Schools Examinations Board (ISEB). You can see their name at the top of each Common Entrance Paper. There are Common Entrance Examinations in every academic subject, and they are an opportunity for you to show Senior School teachers what you can do.

There are two Common Entrance Papers for English: a **Reading paper**, worth 50 marks and lasting 1 hour 10 minutes; and a **Writing paper**, also worth 50 marks and lasting 1 hour 20 minutes.

These papers are made up of the following sections:

Paper 1: READING

SECTION A: NON-FICTION (25 marks)

Here you will be required to answer questions on one or two passages of non-fiction writing. The range of genres for the passages will include (but is not limited to):

- Travel writing (e.g. recounts of journeys, diaries)
- Autobiography or biography
- Journalistic writing (e.g. a newspaper report)
- Persuasive writing (e.g. a speech or long advertisement)
- Discussion text (presenting two or more sides to a particular issue or argument)

There will be approximately five reading comprehension questions. These will test how well you can understand, analyse and evaluate the passage(s).

SECTION B: POETRY (25 marks)

In this section you will be given a poem to read and analyse. This may be a whole poem, or an extract. There may be a clear rhyming scheme or it may be written in blank verse. The subject of the poem could be anything at all, but it is likely that it will be interesting and thought-provoking.

There will be approximately five comprehension questions. These will ask you to respond to the poem in various ways, focusing on how writers achieve their effects, reveal their feelings and make readers more aware. You will need to know about: metaphor, simile, personification, alliteration, rhyme, rhythm and metre.

IMPORTANT NOTE: At the time of writing this book, the ISEB is not including a section on fictional prose (e.g. story extracts) in the examination. However, this is a vast and very important part of your English work, and so a unit on prose has been included in this book.

Paper 2: WRITING

SECTION A: RESPONSE TO STUDIED LITERATURE (25 marks)

Here you will be presented with a choice of four essay questions, based on the literature you have studied in class or read at home, and from which you must choose **one** only.

Two of the questions available will be on a set theme (e.g. relationships, conflict, heroes and heroines). The remaining two questions will be open literature questions, with no particular theme.

In each case, you will be required to show your knowledge of one or more texts, by referring to key events, characters and dramatic moments that relate to the question you have chosen. Your opinions are important and you will need to be able to express them – and justify them – clearly, in the form of a discursive essay.

You should aim to spend about 40 minutes on this section.

SECTION B: RESPONSE TO WRITING TASK (25 marks)

In this section you will be given six writing tasks, from which you must choose **one** only.

The range of tasks available will be broad and will probably include (but will not be limited to) the following types of writing:

- Descriptive (e.g. descriptive passages from stories)
- Discursive (e.g. looking at both sides of an issue or current affairs topic)
- Personal (e.g. writing about your memories, or expressing your thoughts and opinions on a given topic)
- Persuasive (e.g. a debate speech proposing or opposing a given motion)
- Narrative (e.g. storywriting)

Any plans that you write will not be handed in. You should aim to spend about 40 minutes on this section.

How to use this book

English for Common Entrance is a complete guide to all you need to know in order to pass the Common Entrance English Examinations.

It covers each of the above components, in the order in which they appear in the real exams, beginning with how to study non-fiction, and ending with how to write narrative compositions.

Each unit opens with a general introduction and then follows with a collection of chapters, each one based on a different genre, and including:

- individual study skills and advice
- sample passages, model essays or compositions
- Common Entrance practice questions
- extension work
- suggestions for wider reading

You don't have to read this book like a novel, from beginning to end. It is more likely that your teacher will ask you to dip into it – to focus on a particular type of writing and then practise answering questions on it, using the material in this book.

There are lots of interesting extracts, poems, essays and compositions included in this collection. Read and enjoy each one, take notice of the advice that accompanies it and try to answer the questions as fully as you can.

With the help of this book you will be able to show the teachers in your future school just what you are capable of, when you try!

Reading

UNIT 1
STUDYING NON-FICTION

INTRODUCTION

If works of fiction involve settings, characters and events that have been invented by the writer, and as such are imaginary, then non-fictional writing involves the views and experiences of real people, and provides us with factual information about the real places and objects that surround us.

Non-fiction can have many different effects on us as readers. It can influence our thoughts, stimulate our imagination, persuade us, inform us, excite us and even anger us.

AUDIENCE

Non-fiction texts are always written for a specific **audience** – and this may be one person or thousands – millions even. When writers know for whom they are writing, they may select words and phrases that will especially appeal to their target audience. Language can be used in such a way that it will have a specific impact on the reader.

●●● EXERCISE 1

Can you think of some examples of non-fiction writing? Look at the list below. Copy out each item in the list and write the words 'fiction' or 'non-fiction' in brackets next to each one.

a) a newspaper report
b) an autobiography
c) a short story
d) a holiday brochure
e) a playscript
f) a speech
g) a travel journal

●●● EXERCISE 2

Look at the list below of types of non-fiction texts. Think about the people for whom each text might have been written. Discuss your ideas with a partner and then make a list together of the target audience for each one.

a) an estate agent's house particulars
b) a travel company's holiday brochure
c) a journalist's newspaper report
d) a doctor's medical report
e) a theatre critic's review
f) a politician's speech
g) a chef's recipe
h) a footballer's autobiography

PURPOSE

Whenever a writer puts pen to paper, he or she will not only consider the audience for whom they are writing: they will also think about the **purpose** of their writing.

Different non-fiction texts serve many different purposes. Some are examples are:

- to **recount** an event, journey or other experience
- to **report** the news
- to **persuade** readers to think or act in a particular way
- to **discuss** an issue, presenting both sides of an argument
- to **review** a product

● ● ● EXERCISE 3

Can you think of some examples of non-fiction texts that serve these different purposes? Have you read any?

Copy out the above list and next to each bullet point, give at least one example of a text that achieves this purpose.

In a Common Entrance examination you will be given a short extract from a non-fiction text – it may be any one of the above types – and you will then be asked questions based on it. Knowing the audience and purpose of the sample text you have been given will help you to establish how the author has used language to appeal to the reader. You will be able to identify how the **layout** and the **language features** of a text combine to create an impact on the reader.

LAYOUT

The way that a non-fiction text is laid out on the page will have an impact on the reader. For example, a travel recount will be set out in the order in which the journey took place, with times, place names and photographs along the way. Designers of holiday brochures must think carefully about how clear the text is and how attractive the images are.

LANGUAGE FEATURES

Every piece of non-fiction, whether it is a newspaper report, a travel recount or a political speech, will have certain language features that are common to that particular type of text, or genre. For example, an **autobiography** will usually have some or all of the following language features:

- Separate **paragraphs**: to introduce the author's feelings about a particular part of their life, to retell a particular incident, from their own viewpoint, or to show how this incident affected their life
- the **first person narrative** throughout (*I had scarcely...*)
- **descriptive language** to express the author's feelings and attitudes
- **prepositions** and **connectives** to show chronological order (e.g. *then*, *when*, *after*, *thereafter*)
- personal **pronouns** (*me*, *them*, *us*)
- possessive **adjectives** (*my*, *our*, *his*)

The way that language is used – the sorts of features you will find – in a non-fiction text is influenced by its audience and purpose. For example, if the purpose of a speech is to persuade people to vote for the speaker, then he or she will include lots of persuasive adjectives to make them sound appealing (*trustworthy*, *caring*, *reliable*) and imperatives to tell the audience what to do (*listen*, *believe*, *vote for me!*).

●●● EXERCISE 4

What sort of language features do you think you might find in an estate agent's house particulars? You will need to think about its audience and purpose and then make a list of the sorts of words, phrases and techniques you would expect to find in this persuasive text.

RANGE OF TEXTS

As you progress through this unit, you will encounter a range of different non-fiction texts, including:

- a travel recount
- an autobiography
- a newspaper report
- a holiday brochure
- a discussion text
- a film review

In each case you will be asked to think about audience, purpose, layout and language features.

Remember: knowing why, how and for whom a text was written will enable you to step into the author's shoes and picture what they intended when they put pen to paper – and there are many Common Entrance questions that ask you to do just that.

Most importantly, as you gain more experience in studying non-fiction texts, you will become a more **critical reader**, able to spot the features of different texts and to distinguish between facts and opinions, truths and exaggerations.

...and with luck, you'll gain some good exam grades too!

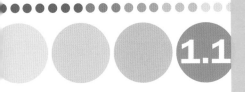

Language
Features

 Discussion

A good **travel writer** uses words ~~in the same way that they~~ use a camera – to capture image~~s of a place so that visitors~~ that others can imagine what it ~~was like, without ever visiting it for~~ themselves.

Have you ever returned from a holiday with lots of stories to tell, and then enjoyed sharing them with a friend or relative? This is what travel writers do. They carefully observe all the sights and sounds they encounter when they are in a distant place: the people, the wildlife, the landscape, the weather. Then they describe them in detail using lots of descriptive language.

Good travel writing captures the imagination; it enables readers to explore distant lands that they may never have the chance to see for themselves. Travel writing broadens minds.

But how do travel writers manage to keep their readers interested? Why, after all, should we want to hear about someone else's travel adventures? What makes a good **travel recount**?

 Focus

AUDIENCE AND PURPOSE

- Travel recounts are written for readers who may or may not have visited the particular place being described, but are interested to learn more about it. Some may then choose to travel there for themselves; others may just enjoy 'escaping' for a few moments on an imaginary journey.
- The general purpose of travel writing is to paint a vivid picture of a destination, or journey, using descriptive language. Some travel writing may persuade readers to journey to a particular destination – as in a holiday brochure. Other purposes include: to review a place or venue, or to recount the stages of an epic journey (see the sample on page 7).

> ● ● ● EXERCISE 1
>
> ~~Th~~ink for a moment about ~~th~~e places you have visited ~~on~~ a holiday. How would ~~yo~~u describe them in ~~wo~~rds? Can you remember some of the sights, sounds and smells you encountered when you were there?
>
> Focus on one particular destination in your mind and then describe this place to a partner. Remember that your listener wasn't on holiday with you, so your description will need to be vivid and interesting.

> ● ● ● EXERCISE 2
>
> Have you ever been somewhere for a holiday that you did not enjoy? What did you dislike about the place? Share your feelings about the destination with a friend.
>
> Have you ever been on an interesting journey? How did you travel: by land, sea or air? Share with your class some of the experiences you encountered along the way.

LAYOUT

- Travel writing is usually written in full prose – that is to say, sentences and paragraphs rather than bullet points or short notes.
- Usually travel writing will introduce the reader to a particular place or stage of a journey in the opening paragraph and then proceed to describe its features. If the travel writing has been written as a journal – or travel diary – then the account will be written in chronological order, describing the sights and sounds as the writer encountered them.
- Photographs and maps are often included to help readers picture the locations visited.

LANGUAGE FEATURES

Travel writing often includes:

- **facts and figures** referring to land features, climate, communities, local history and so on
- **first person narrative** – using 'I' and 'me' rather than the third person narrative – to show that the writer is speaking from his or her own point of view and recounting a personal experience
- **descriptive language** – vivid and interesting adjectives, adverbs, metaphors and similes to bring the place to life and enable readers to imagine it in their mind's eye
- **personal thoughts and reflections** of the writer, sharing how they felt when they were visiting the place and prompting us to imagine how we might feel in the same situation.

Remember: as a travel writer, you can never assume that your readers have been to the place you are describing, so your description must be clear and colourful – try to make it even better than a photograph!

●●● EXERCISE 3

Think back to the holiday destination you described to your partner earlier in the lesson. Can you think of some interesting adjectives you could use to sum up the people, the landscape and the climate?

Write these down and then share them with your class.

See if you can identify some of the key features of travel writing in the sample below.

 # Sample

Michael Palin is well known for his epic travels across the globe. Here, in an excerpt from Pole to Pole, *he describes his epic journey from Awasa to Moyale, in Ethopia.*

●●● DAY 86: Lake Awasa to Moyale

Scatter the monkeys from the vehicles at 7 o'clock as we load up once again. It's our eleventh day in Ethiopia. By tonight we hope to be in the border town of Moyale, 325
5   miles away. We pick our way through the Awasa rush hour, in which we are about the only vehicles. Everyone else is walking; schoolchildren, farmers, soldiers, workers on their way to the textile factory or the
10   production lines of the National Tobacco and Matches Corporation.

    There is not much public transport down here. People either walk, or pack into the back of precarious and over-laden pick-up trucks, which travel at lethal speeds. There is the occasional bus, so occasional that it is usually packed to the gunnels. The only other alternative is to hitch
15   a ride on top of a truck. This sounds to me a novel way of seeing Africa, which is why I end up jostling with banana sellers in the main road at Yirga Alem at 9 o'clock on a Thursday morning. After a half-hour wait we persuade a small truck packed with sacks of kef to take us some of the way to Moyale.

    The roadside buzzes with life on this stretch of green, fertile, lushly tropical valley, and besides
20   the usual firewood and charcoal vendors are small children waving sugar canes four times their own size, and squatting figures laying out white peanuts to dry on the hot road surface.

    Pedestrians – mostly women – toil by with enormous loads on backs or heads. A mountain of cut grass almost obscures the old lady beneath it, giving the impression that it is moving up the road of its own volition.

25   ...By early afternoon the countryside has changed from the fertile valleys to a scrub-covered semi-desert. I've seen camels for the first time since the Sudan and the termite architecture is increasingly Gothic. One mound, at least 15 feet high, is the most extraordinary feat of building I have seen since the Hypostyle Hall at Karnak.

    The people are changing too. We are now in the land of the Borena, animists and gatherers.
30   The women are very beautiful, exotically dressed in bright swirls of jade green, deep blue and lemon yellow. They smile broadly as we pass.

    At 5.30 a rattling truck takes us through the last of the army checkpoints and into the town of Moyale.

From *Pole to Pole* by Michael Palin (BBC Books, 1992)
Reprinted by permission of The Random House Group Ltd.

●●● EXERCISE 4

Who do you think this account is aimed at?

What is the purpose of Palin's article? What is he hoping to achieve by writing it?

Find several language features in the excerpt that help to make the scene come alive for readers at home. Which words and phrases are the most vivid for you?

? Questions

1   How many hours does it take for Palin to travel from Asawa to Moyale?

2   Describe the ways in which the rush hour in Asawa is different from the rush hours Palin would be used to in England.

3   Put the following phrase into your own words, retaining the same meaning as far as possible: 'precarious and over-laden pick-up trucks' (line 13).

4   Without public transport, how do most people get about?

5a) Based on your reading of the passage, list five different sounds that you think Palin might have heard during his time in Asawa?

 b) List two different smells that Palin may have encountered in Asawa.

6   Describe in your own words how the landscape on Palin's journey has changed by the afternoon.

7   Do you think Palin enjoyed the second half of his day trip more than the first? How can you tell?

⟷ Extension

8   What impressions do you get from the passage about what life is like for the people who live and work in Asawa? Refer to the text in your answer.

9   Re-read the passage again. Then write an imaginary postcard which Palin might have sent to his family in England, in which he describes his journey from Asawa to Moyale.

10 Using evidence from the passage, write a short extract that might appear in a children's geography textbook, or encyclopaedia, on Ethiopia. Describe the town of Asawa – its location and its people. Remember: you are now writing in the **third person**, giving **factual information** rather than personal opinions.

📖 Wider Reading

11 Research the country of Ethiopia. You may refer to geography textbooks, encyclopaedias and atlases in school, or use internet sites such as the following:

www.13suns.com

www.plan-uk.org/wherewework/
    eastafricaeurope/ethiopia

Share what you have found with your class, and then compile a display or classbook.

12 Find out more about Michael Palin's globe-trotting adventures. His journeys have been turned into television series, with books to accompany them. These include: *Around the World in Eighty Days* (BBC Books, 2004), *Pole to Pole* (BBC Books, 2004), *Sahara* (Phoenix Press, 2003) and *Himalaya* (Phoenix Press, 2005). You can find out more by visiting: www.palinstravels.co.uk

Discussion

An **autobiography** is the personal account of someone's life. Written in the first person, it shares the writer's experiences, describing the people they encountered and the places they visited – all from the writer's own viewpoint. Autobiographies allow us to 'tell our own story'.

A **biography** is also the story of one person's life, but it is not written by the person whose life is being recounted, so the third person narrative is used. Biographies can be equally interesting for the reader, as they include the thoughts and feelings of many other people in the subject's life.

Autobiographies and biographies can reveal how famous people have found success. Often readers find it has not been an easy ride for them.

Autobiographies can offer readers a glimpse into the private lives of public figures. They show us what makes a person who they are – how their life has been shaped, and by whom. Autobiographies tell true stories that may be happy, sad, amusing or inspirational, but are always interesting.

Focus

AUDIENCE AND PURPOSE

- Autobiographies are written for readers who may have heard of the writer and would like to find out more about their life.
- The purpose of an autobiography is to record the events and experiences encountered in the writer's life, and to describe these from the writer's own viewpoint, sharing their personal thoughts and feelings along the way.

● ● ● EXERCISE 1

Is there a famous person whom you admire? Perhaps a sporting hero, an artist, or an actor? Have you ever wondered how they got to where they are today? In small groups, share your views on whom you admire, and why.

Would you like to know more about them? Choose one particular person and make a list of questions you would like to ask them – about their life, their influences and how they got to where they are today.

● ● ● EXERCISE 2

Many autobiographies begin at the beginning, when the writer was a child. What is your earliest memory? Find a partner to work with and then take turns in recounting some of your earliest childhood memories.

Since beginning school, what have been your major achievements? Have there been any school events and experiences in particular that have left a big impression on you? Why? Would you put them in your autobiography?

LAYOUT AND STRUCTURE

- Autobiographies (and biographies) are written in full **prose** – sentences and paragraphs.
- Autobiographies are usually written in **chronological order**, beginning with the writer's childhood experiences and then progressing through their life, with significant events along the way.
- **Descriptive**, **complex sentences** are often included, allowing the writer to combine factual accounts of events with descriptive phrases that reveal their thoughts and feelings at the time.

LANGUAGE FEATURES

Autobiographies usually include:

- use of the **first person narrative** – using 'I' and 'me' rather than the third person narrative ('he' or 'she'), to express the writer's own point of view
- **time references and factual** details to show when, where and why events have taken place
- **personal thoughts and reflections** of the writer, in response to the events and experiences they encounter during their life
- **descriptive language** throughout, including adjectives, adverbs, similes and metaphors

● ● ● EXERCISE 3

Choose one particular event that has been memorable for you in the last year – perhaps a sports day, a school play or an exciting family holiday. Write some notes about the event, listing where and when it took place and how you felt at the time.

Autobiographies are particularly interesting when they tell the story of someone who has overcome hardship or difficulty to find happiness and success in later life.

 Sample

Winston Churchill is often regarded as our greatest Prime Minister. He steered the country to a famous victory in the Second World War. But, as his autobiography shows, he found the challenge of school very difficult.

I had scarcely passed my twelfth birthday when I entered the inhospitable regions of examinations, through which for the next seven years I was destined to journey. These examinations were a great trial to me. The 5 subjects which were dearest to the examiners were almost invariably those I fancied least. I would have liked to have been examined in history, poetry and writing essays. The examiners, on the other hand, were partial to 10 Latin and mathematics. And their will prevailed. Moreover, the questions which they asked on both these subjects were almost invariably those to which I was unable to suggest a satisfactory answer. I should have liked to be asked to say what I knew. They always tried to ask what I did not know. When I would have willingly displayed my knowledge, they sought to expose 15 my ignorance. This sort of treatment had only one result: I did not do well in examinations.

This was especially true of my Entrance Examination to Harrow. The Head-master, Mr. Welldon, however, took a broad-minded view of my Latin prose: he showed discernment in judging my general ability. This was the more remarkable, because I was found unable to answer a single question in the Latin paper. I wrote my name at the top of the page. I wrote down the number of 20 the question '1'. After much reflection I put a bracket around it thus '(1)'. But thereafter I could not think of anything connected with it that was either relevant or true. Incidentally there arrived from nowhere in particular a blot and several smudges. I gazed for two whole hours at this sad spectacle: and then merciful ushers collected my piece of foolscap with all the others and carried it up to the Head-master's table. It was from these slender indications of scholarship that Mr. 25 Welldon drew the conclusion that I was worthy to pass into Harrow. It is very much to his credit. It showed that he was a man capable of looking beneath the surface of things: a man not dependent upon paper manifestations. I have always had the greatest regard for him.

In consequence of his decision, I was in due course placed in the third, or lowest, division of the Fourth, or bottom, Form. The names of the new boys were printed in the School List in 30 alphabetical order; and as my correct name, Spencer-Churchill, began with an 'S', I gained no more advantage from the alphabet than from the wider sphere of letters. I was in fact only two from the bottom of the whole school; and these two, I regret to say, disappeared almost immediately through illness or some other cause.

From *My Early Life* by Winston Churchill (Thornton Butterworth, 1934)

Who do you think the above passage was written for? Who might be interested in reading Churchill's memoirs?

Why do you think Churchill chose to write about this experience in his life particularly?

Look again at the language features often found in autobiographies. Can you identify similar features in this passage?

? Questions

1 What is meant by the phrase 'inhospitable regions'? (line 2)

2 How do you think Churchill regards the system of school exams? Explain your answer with close reference to the text.

3 What are the reasons Churchill gives for failing?

4 In a few lines, describe Churchill's efforts in the Latin examination at Harrow, from the point of view of a teacher or usher, present in the room.

5 How did Churchill come to be at the very bottom of the school register?

6 Churchill describes Mr Welldon as 'a man capable of looking beneath the surface of things' (line 27). What do you think he means by this?

7 What impression do you get of young Winston's character from the passage? What sort of pupil do you think he was? Support your comments with specific references to the text.

⟷ Extension

8 Imagine that Churchill is invited back to Harrow some years later to talk to the pupils about how to cope with examinations. What sort of advice would he offer them? Write down an imaginary speech he might give to his young audience on the subject of school exams. Use the first person narrative.

9 Write a short playscript involving a twelve-year-old Churchill and his father, in which they discuss Winston's poor efforts in the Entrance Examination for Harrow. What will his father say? How will Churchill excuse his own behaviour?

10 What do you think of school examinations? Are they a 'necessary evil', i.e. something that is unpleasant but important all the same? Produce a short piece of personal writing in which you share your opinion and experience of school examinations.

📖 Wider Reading

11 Find out more about the life and work of Winston Churchill. There have been many books written about him, including several biographies. Useful websites include the following:

www.spartacus.schoolnet.co.uk/
    PRchurchill.htm

www.bbc.co.uk/history/historic_figures/
    churchill_winston.shtml

www.churchill-society-london.org.uk

12 Read the autobiographies of other famous people. Some recommended books are:

Black, White & Gold: My Autobiography by Kelly Holmes (Virgin, 2006)

David Attenborough: Life on Air by David Attenborough (BBC Books, 2003)

Martin Johnson Autobiography by Martin Johnson (Headline, 2004)

Taking on the World by Ellen MacArthur (Michael Joseph, 2002)

Steve Redgrave: The Golden Age by Steve Redgrave and Nick Townsend (BBC Books, 2001)

Boy: Tales of Childhood and Going Solo by Roald Dahl (Puffin, 2001)

Discussion

Journalistic reports – also known as **newspaper reports** – give us written versions of the daily news.

Journalistic texts tell us about events that have taken place, decisions that have been made and situations that have arisen, all of which may affect us in some way.

Some journalistic texts may be in the form of a recount, giving a chronological commentary on an event that has taken place, like a royal wedding, or a military campaign. Other texts may be written as a report, announcing an important news item and then recording people's responses to it.

News can be very serious, and life-changing for all those involved, like a natural disaster or a war being fought. But it can also be light-hearted and trivial, like celebrity gossip or news of a latest fashion trend.

Whether they are writing about serious issues or not, journalists try to give their readers a truthful account of what is happening around them. Even today, with the vast range of multimedia systems at our fingertips, newspapers continue to play an important role in our lives.

Focus

AUDIENCE AND PURPOSE

- Audience: Newspapers are read by anyone and everyone. Some specific news stories may be of particular interest to some people more than others, especially if they are involved in the news event, but many people just like to know what is happening in the world around them.
- Purpose: The function of journalistic texts is to report the news – whatever and wherever it may be. Readers should be able to learn what is going on in the world, without having to travel the globe themselves.

●●● EXERCISE 1

How often do you read newspaper reports? What sort of news do you like to read about – sport, music, world news, film and television or politics?

Are you up to date with what is happening in the world around you? What has the news been like recently? With a partner, discuss any news stories you may have heard or read about in the last week. Then share these with your class.

●●● EXERCISE 2

Working with a partner, make a list of the different types of news stories you may find in a national daily newspaper. You don't need to mention specific news items – just the kinds of events you might expect to read about.

LAYOUT

- Journalistic reports often use a combination of bold headlines, computer images or photographs. They comprise written prose, laid out in proper sentences and short paragraphs, for ease of reading.
- The text in a newspaper is usually set out in narrow columns, again to enable readers to scan each report quickly. Accompanying images usually have captions written below them.

LANGUAGE FEATURES

Most journalistic reports include:

- use of the **third person narrative** and the **passive voice** to create an impartial, formal account of the news (e.g. *soldiers were seen entering the building*)
- use of the **past tense** to describe events that have already taken place (unlike a television report that may be 'live at the scene' as events are unfolding)
- some word play, including **alliteration**, particularly in headlines, to capture readers' attention and engage their interest
- **reported** and **direct speech** to convey the thoughts and reactions of interested parties and experts in the field
- **journalistic terms and phrases** that are rarely found in other situations, like '*the Minister was unavailable for comment*' and '*sources close to the Prime Minister said...*'

The way that a newspaper report is written – its tone and slant – can affect how readers react to the news that it conveys. This means that journalists have quite considerable power and responsibility. Some newspapers may even present the news in a way that favours certain beliefs or political persuasions.

SAMPLE

In the following excerpt from The Independent, *scientists discover a new ancestor for us all.*

THE 3FT-TALL 'HOBBIT' THAT REWRITES THE HISTORY OF MANKIND

'This is the most exciting surprise to hit anthropology for decades.' – **Richard Dawkins**

SCIENTISTS are celebrating the most important breakthrough in anthropology for
5 a century: the discovery of a new species of apeman.

Described as human 'hobbits' the apemen grew no taller than about 3ft and had brains the size of grapefruits. They lived alongside
10 prehistoric man for thousands of years before they finally died out in the dense jungles of Indonesia, in a lost world inhabited by dwarf elephants and giant rats.

Archaeologists excavated the skeletal remains
15 of the little humans from a cave on the remote Indonesian island of Flores, which has a rich history of exotic animals such as giant lizards and miniature beasts.

Four dating techniques proved the species of
20 'little people' was still living in the region as recently as 13,000 years ago. They may even have survived modern times – when they could have been the inspiration for local folktales of shy pygmy apemen who lived in the forest.

25 Specialists said the new species, officially named *Homofloresiensis*, or Flores Man, calls into question the very nature of what it means to be human, because of its extraordinary dwarfed features and tiny brain.

30 A partial skeleton of a female, nicknamed 'hobbit' by the research team, has left the specialists in no doubt that Flores Woman represents a new and most unusual member of the human family. The skeleton is 18,000 years old and, although
35 small, is perfectly proportioned.

At first, researchers thought she was a child but closed skull sutures and wear on the teeth suggest that she was about 30 when she died. Further remains of up to seven individuals,
40 some dating to only 13,000 years ago, suggest that there was once a thriving population on the volcanic island.

It is unequivocal evidence that another species of human was living at the same time
45 as our recent ancestors. It suggests the two would almost certainly have come into contact with one another at some time.

The zoologist and writer Richard Dawkins, professor of scientific understanding at
50 Oxford University, described the find as 'the most exciting surprise to hit anthropology for decades'.

Article by Steve Connor & David Keys in
The Independent, Thursday 28 October 2004

Towards whom do you think this article is aimed? Describe its target audience.

What is the purpose of this report? Can you summarise the key points of news that it conveys?

Remind yourself of the language features common to newspaper reports. Can you identify any of them here?

❓ Questions

1 Why do you think the news report opens with the quotation from Richard Dawkins? What effect does it have?

2 How does the phrase 'human "hobbits"' contribute to our understanding of the new species? (line 7)

3 What evidence is there to suggest that these 'little people' might have survived until modern times?

4 Why does this discovery call into question what it means to be human?

5 How did the species come to be named Flores Man?

6 Throughout the news article, the writer draws comparisons with everyday objects and images, in order to help our understanding of the size and the appearance of the apemen. Write down two examples of these comparisons and say how effective each one is.

7 Why should this discovery be so important? Explain your answer as fully as you can and with reference to the passage.

↔ Extension

8 Write a précis (short summary) of this newspaper report, in no more than 50 words.

9 Imagine you are one of the archaeologists working on the island. You are responsible for finding the remains of the Flores Woman. Record your thoughts and feelings about the remarkable discovery in a journal. Begin by describing how you came to find the remains.

10 Write your own newspaper report about a similar find – fictional or real – in which archaeologists make a momentous discovery that could change the way we think about evolution. You might choose a new type of dinosaur, for example, or the remains of a giant human. Think carefully about the layout and language features you will use.

📖 Wider Reading

11 There are many different types of newspaper, and these reflect the different audiences who read them. Compare and contrast the style and news content of two very different newspapers – for example *The Sun* and the *Daily Telegraph*. What do you notice? Record your observations and share them with your class.

12 Find out more about the extraordinary story of Flores Man. See if you can find other news reports on the same subject. You will find that most newspapers have their own websites, in which past news reports are archived. For example:

http://news.independent.co.uk
www.timesonline.co.uk

Discussion

Persuasive texts come in many shapes and sizes, from one-line slogans on a billboard to full length political speeches. In all cases, language is being used to *persuade* readers (or listeners) to think or act in a particular way.

You can see persuasive texts all around you – in magazines and newspapers, in shop windows and railway stations – and you can hear persuasive texts being read aloud, in television and radio advertisements, and in the speeches of politicians, church leaders and company executives.

For every persuasive text, a particular audience is targeted and words and phrases are selected for their special appeal. A range of language techniques are used in order to create the biggest impact on the reader – to persuade them to buy a product, register a vote or join a protest, for example.

 Focus

AUDIENCE AND PURPOSE

- Persuasive texts are usually written for a specific or 'target' audience: readers and/or listeners who may or may not know much about the subject of the text, but wish to find out more before making a decision or choice.
- The purpose of any persuasive text is to present a product or a point of view to the target audience and persuade them to act in a particular way as a result – by spending money or supporting a cause, for example.

●●● EXERCISE 1

With a partner, think for a few moments about the sorts of persuasive texts you have seen or heard recently.

Make a list of examples and then share them with your class. Consider together what these texts may have in common.

●●● EXERCISE 2

What other purposes can you think of for persuasive texts? What can they achieve?

Working in a pair or small group, make a list of the different reasons why you might want to write a persuasive text. What do you want your readers to do? Some examples to begin with are:

- to buy a product
- to book a holiday
- to support a charity

LAYOUT

- Persuasive texts often begin with a headline or a slogan that catches readers' attention
- Then there will usually be a punchy, exciting opening paragraph, which introduces a product or presents a viewpoint
- Longer persuasive texts, like brochures and speeches, may be divided up into separate paragraphs, each one introducing a new feature, or extending an argument
- Eye-catching artwork may be included, with accompanying annotations and captions

LANGUAGE FEATURES

Most persuasive texts include:

- **rich descriptions** (also called 'emotive language') to influence the reader's thoughts and feelings – e.g. powerful adjectives, adverbs, similes and metaphors
- **comparatives and superlatives** to emphasise the positive aspects of a product or the strengths of an argument – e.g. *better prices*, *the most beautiful scenery*, *the best way*
- **alliteration** and **onomatopoeia** to improve the appeal and sound of the text and engage the reader's imagination – e.g. *Soft, silky sand*
- **imperatives** to engage readers' attention and invite them to sample a product, or think in a particular way – e.g. *relax and unwind*, *drive in luxury* or *join us today*
- **rhetorical questions:** these are questions to which the answers may seem obvious – e.g. *Want to get rid of stress?* or *Want to find happiness?*

Remember: persuasive texts use a combination of all these language features and techniques to reach out to readers and influence their feelings. In this way they may often use the kind of writing we see in stories – or even poetry – where words and phrases on a page can actually affect the way we feel.

●●● EXERCISE 3

Have you ever been persuaded by an advertisement or a holiday brochure?

Has a speech that someone has delivered ever changed the way you think about something?

Share your experiences with a friend.

Sample

The following passage is from the website of a travel company selling luxury holidays.
Will you be persuaded to take a trip to America after reading it?

USA – Western States: Wonderful Wild West

The western states of the USA have an abundance of some of the most spectacular natural sightseeing in the world, from the blue waters and rugged coastline of California to the barren deserts of Arizona and Nevada. 5

If you are looking to visit cosmopolitan cities, Los Angeles and San Francisco are excellent choices, while those wanting to take in some stunning scenery can visit one of the many National Parks. 10

Take a plane over the breathtaking Grand Canyon, enjoy the excitement and glamour of Las Vegas or simply unwind on a Californian beach, the options are virtually endless. To explore as much of this region as possible, you can tailor make your own itinerary on one of our fly drive holidays or take one of our escorted 15 coach tours.

Los Angeles: The city of angels

Los Angeles is a huge sprawling city that borders the Pacific Ocean. From the slopes of the rich and famous on Rodeo Drive to the life guards on Venice Beach, L.A. has it all. Don't miss the city's great attractions – Universal Studios, the Sunset Strip, Hollywood, Beverley Hills and Disneyland. 20

Stay close to the Pacific, at Marina del Rey, and explore Venice Beach or Santa Monica, or mix with the stars in Beverley Hills or Hollywood. It's a city where the car rules. The freedom of a rental car is recommended to get around and explore.

Las Vegas: Glitz and Glamour

Viva Las Vegas – One of America's most visited destinations is an all year round playground in the Nevada desert. Las Vegas is glitz, glamour and must be seen to be believed. The city is open 25 24 hours a day for entertainment, dining or gambling in the many casinos.

During the day, relax by the pool of your hotel, or take a tour of the Grand Canyon which is a short flight away. And at night, see the spectacular Fremont Street experience, one of the many top class shows or just gamble your hard earned money away.

From *www.kuoni.co.uk*

●●● EXERCISE 4

What sort of reader might be interested in this article?

What is Kuoni hoping to achieve by writing it?

Can you find any evidence to show that the writer has tried to make an impact on the reader? Do you notice any of those persuasive language features here?

? Questions

1 In what ways do the western states cater for the holidaymaker looking for peace and quiet?

2 Find two examples of alliteration in use in the passage and describe the effect each one might have on the reader.

3 Give three reasons why the city of Los Angeles is so famous.

4 The claim 'L.A. has it all' (line 18) is a proud boast. To what extent do you think it is justified by what the reader is told in this article? Explain your answer as fully as you can.

5 Explain fully what is meant by the phrase 'all year round playground' (line 24) when talking about Las Vegas.

6 How does the photograph enhance the impact this article might have on readers? What does it bring to the passage?

7 Write an imaginary postcard which you might send home whilst on holiday enjoying a tour of the western states of America. Describe your thoughts and feelings about the places you have seen and the experiences you have had.

←→ Extension

8 Write the script for a short television advertisement which advertises Kuoni holidays in the USA's western states. Include as many destinations and experiences as you can and remember to use language that is punchy and exciting, to persuade the viewers to book a holiday with Kuoni.

9 An elderly relative of yours likes to enjoy quiet holidays in unspoilt countryside. She has heard that there is some beautiful scenery along the western side of America and asks if you know anything about this part of the USA. Will you recommend it to her? Write your conversation as a playscript.

10 Choose a favourite holiday destination that you have visited with your family. Write an excerpt from an imaginary holiday brochure, in which you promote the destination as the place to go for a dream holiday.
You may wish to consider:
● layout
● language features
● the attractions and facilities on offer
● the type of holiday you are advertising
● whom your target audience might be

📖 Wider Reading

11 Research internet websites, books, magazines and brochures to locate other examples of persuasive writing, including:
● an estate agent's particulars
● a car manufacturer's latest catalogue
● a school prospectus
For each example, look out for the language features and techniques that are common to most persuasive texts.

12 Visit the following website, which contains some very famous speeches:
www.famousquotes.me.uk/speeches
Choose one speech in particular and write down some thoughts in response to it. Has it changed the way you think in some way? Are you persuaded by what the speaker has to say?

Discussion

Discussion texts are pieces of writing that make you think. Sometimes called discursive articles, they appear in magazines, newspapers, books and online. Discussion texts present fresh ideas, different opinions and new theories to be challenged.

When you read a discursive article you may find yourself agreeing or disagreeing with what has been written, but you will always be prompted to form an opinion of some kind. Opposing arguments and views will be presented to you and it is for you to decide what you think.

There are usually two sides to every issue and a good discussion text presents both points of view in a clear and balanced way. To produce a discursive text you need good listening skills, so that you can find out what people think and then write down their thoughts as accurately as you can.

Focus

AUDIENCE AND PURPOSE

- The issues that are discussed in discursive articles may appeal to some people more than others, so the headline is important. Discursive articles often appear in magazines and newspaper supplements at weekends, when readers have more time to think about the issues being raised.
- The purpose of discursive articles is to raise awareness about a certain issue and to present both sides of the argument, allowing readers to form a balanced and informed opinion for themselves.

●●● EXERCISE 1

What sort of issues might you find in a discussion text? Can you think of any controversial issues in the news today that provoke a range of different viewpoints and opinions?

Make a list of controversial issues that sometimes cause disagreement. Some examples include: nuclear power, wind farms, fox-hunting and using animals for research.

●●● EXERCISE 2

Working with a partner, choose one specific issue, like fox-hunting for example, and write down as much as you can on both sides of the debate. Then take a position each – one person for and the other against – and debate the issue, listening and responding sensibly to each other's views.

LAYOUT

- Discussion texts usually begin by introducing the issue to be discussed. This might be a controversial building plan, or a new law being proposed, for example.
- After the introduction, different views will be presented and direct quotations may be included, from people who have an interest in the issue being discussed.
- Sometimes a conclusion – or editorial – is written at the end of the piece, which will summarise the different views held and may present the writer's own final words.
- Use of visual images and graphics enhances the text and provides readers with additional information on the given topic.

LANGUAGE FEATURES

A discussion text often includes:

- use of the third person narrative, to create an impartial and balanced voice
- connectives that allow the writer to switch between different viewpoints and connect and sequence ideas – e.g. however, on the other hand
- use of the present tense, to present views that are held now – e.g. some believe, others disagree
- words and phrases that suggest opinion and beliefs rather than facts – e.g. probably, maybe, there are those that believe
- direct and reported speech to record accurately the opposing views of people on both sides

Discussion texts present different opinions and views. When you are reading them, and forming your own opinions, you need to be careful to distinguish **facts** from **opinions**. Assess the strength of the arguments offered and always check to see if claims are supported by strong evidence.

Sample

In the following excerpt from the Northern Echo, *new plans to build a giant wind farm receive a mixed response.*

IN THE LAND OF THE GIANTS

A planning inquiry into a Cumbrian windfarm is being watched with interest by campaigners in the North-East.

The public inquiry into an application for 27 wind turbines at Whinash, near Tebay at Penrith, Cumbria, began yesterday and is expected to last five weeks.

The development would be the largest land turbine development in Europe, measuring more than five miles in length.

It has been backed by environmental groups including Greenpeace and Friends of the Earth, who say it will help in the battle against climate change.

However, campaigners against the wind farm say the noise and visual impact on the landscape would outweigh its environmental benefits.

The site is near the M6 between the Yorkshire Dales and Lake District National Park.

Jill Perry, energy campaigner for Friends of the Earth, said of the Whinash inquiry: "I am amazed that people are claiming that the area should be designated a national park.

"What kind of national park has a motorway running through it?

"People need to wake up to the fact that climate change will happen and it's not good enough to pretend that we can sit back for the next few years thinking about the situation."

However, Elizabeth Mann, from Darlington, who successfully led a campaign against a windfarm at Barningham High Moor, near Barnard Castle, said the 377ft turbines would have a much greater visual impact than the motorway.

The retired teacher said: "The A66 runs near the Stang Forest (near Barningham) scheme and this was defeated in the High Court.

"The motorway is level with the ground and these turbines are 400ft high, one of them is bigger than the hill it is on.

"I am going to the public inquiry.

"Each site must be looked at specifically and the benefits weighed up against the non-benefits.

"I've walked in Whinash and on balance I think it should be left as it is."

From the *Northern Echo*,
20 April 2005
http://www.darlingtonandstocktontimes.co.uk

● ● ● ● ● **EXERCISE 3**

Who do you think would read this article? Consider where it appeared and what its readership might be.

What is the purpose of this article?

Consider which parts of this passage are direct quotations and which are reported speech. Do you find direct quotations more persuasive?

? Questions

1 Explain in a sentence or two what is being proposed for the site at Whinash.

2 Why do you think this article is entitled 'In the Land of the Giants'? What effect does this headline have on the reader?

3 Why should environmental groups support such a plan?

4 What are the main objections to the wind farm?

5 Why does Jill Perry find the complaints about the wind farm surprising?

6 Why should the wind farm's developers be particularly concerned that Elizabeth Mann is involved in the campaign against their plan?

7 As a local resident, are Elizabeth's views more important than those of Greenpeace and Friends of the Earth campaigners? Explain your answer as fully as you can.

⟷ Extension

8 In the role of Elizabeth Mann, write a short letter to the *Darlington & Stockton Times*, in which you persuade other local residents to join your campaign against the wind farm.

9 Imagine that Jill Perry and Elizabeth Mann are both invited for a 'head-to-head' debate on a local radio station. Write the conversation they might have as a playscript. You will need to include some words from the radio presenter: an introduction to set the scene for listeners and some interesting questions for the guests.

10 Imagine you are a newspaper reporter, sent to Whinash to interview residents and test local reactions to the wind farm plans. You find some mixed reactions to the scheme. Write up these fictional views in a discursive article of your own.

📖 Wider Reading

11 Find out more about wind farms. How does this form of sustainable energy actually work? You can find lots of information in encyclopaedias and magazines, or check out related websites including the following:
www.yes2wind.com
www.rspb.org.uk/policy/windfarms
www.offshorewindfarms.co.uk

12 Research the different views held about nuclear power as an alternative energy source. What are the advantages? Why do people object to it? Once you have enough information, write your own discussion text on the nuclear power debate. The BBC Newsround website is a useful place to find out about nuclear power. Check out their 'Guide to Energy' at
http://news.bbc.co.uk/cbbcnews
(click on 'Guides' in the left-hand column, then 'Energy' in the A–Z listing).

REVIEWS

Discussion

Whenever a new book, play or film is released, it is usually accompanied by a flurry of **reviews**, written by professional or amateur reviewers, known as **critics**.

A good or bad review can mean the difference between success and failure for a playwright or author. Some readers may value what critics say, while others may want to see the film or read the book for themselves and then reach their own conclusions.

Reviews of books and plays are known as **literary reviews**, but there are plenty of other types of review. Virtually everything you can buy today will have been reviewed by someone at some stage – whether it is a new car, a tennis racket or a package holiday to Spain.

Reviews are important because they help us to find out what others think of something before we go ahead and buy it. But remember, reviews are only one person's opinion: you may disagree!

Focus

AUDIENCE AND PURPOSE

- Reviews are written for readers who would like to know more about a new product or piece of work. They may have read the book or watched the film being reviewed, and will be interested to see if they agree with the critic's views. On the other hand, they may be thinking about making a purchase and want to know if it is worth the money.
- The purpose of a review is to provide readers with a balanced, critical evaluation of something, summarising what it is about and then highlighting its good and bad points.

● ● ● EXERCISE 1

Have you ever been to see a film or read a book because it has been recommended to you? Perhaps you have avoided seeing a play because others have criticised it.

Think about a book you have read or a film you have seen recently that you really enjoyed. Share your thoughts with a friend. Why would you recommend it?

● ● ● EXERCISE 2

Think of a product that you or your family has bought recently – perhaps a car, or a computer. Review the product by writing down three positive things about it and three things which you would like to improve on it.

LAYOUT

- Reviews will often begin with a **summary** of what is being reviewed to orientate the reader. This might be the synopsis of a story from a film or a book, or some facts about a product, like the cost and the size.
- A review will be written in proper sentences and paragraphs. Each new paragraph will introduce a different aspect or feature of the product being reviewed – e.g. for a film you might cover the setting, cast, sound track, camera work, script and so on.

LANGUAGE FEATURES

Reviews usually include:

- **factual information** to introduce the reader to the product or piece of work being reviewed
- **descriptive language**, including adjectives, adverbs, similes and metaphors, to describe a product from the critic's own viewpoint
- **connectives** to show time (e.g. *next*, *then*, *later on*, *finally*), especially for a play or story, allowing the critic to lead the reader through from the beginning to the end
- **comparatives** and **superlatives** to enable the critic to give his or her verdict on what is being reviewed (e.g. *better*, *worse*, *funniest*, *most enjoyable*)
- **ratings** – sometimes in the form of a fraction, or a certain number of stars (e.g. *three-star rating*, or *six out of ten*)

Writing a good review may be considered an art form in itself, with its own array of skills and techniques to be mastered.

Remember: a good review will find negative and positive things to say about something. No one wants to read a long list of complaints (unless it is designed to be amusing!).

● ● ● EXERCISE 3

Can you think of different products you have seen or sampled that had star ratings? Perhaps you have visited a five-star hotel, or eaten in a Michelin star restaurant.

Share your thoughts with a partner.

Sample

J. R. R. Tolkien's The Lord of the Rings *is a classic story, loved by millions. When director Peter Jackson decided to turn the book into three films, critics around the world waited to see if he would be successful. See if you agree with the following verdict.*

Reviewer's rating: ★★★★

The Lord of the Rings: The Fellowship of the Ring (2001)

Funny, scary and, totally involving, Peter Jackson's assured adaptation of JRR Tolkien's The Lord of the Rings turns the book's least screen-worthy volume into a gripping and powerful adventure movie.   5

For the first hour, 'The Fellowship of the Ring' is a flawless introduction to the world of Middle-earth, expertly outlining the backstory and evoking a tangible sense of danger as Frodo the hobbit (Wood) sets out on his quest to destroy the all-powerful one ring – sought-after weapon of the Dark Lord Sauron. **With the wizard Gandalf (McKellen) as his guide – and a protective fellowship drawn   10 from various Middle-earth races – Frodo must do battle with orcs and other beasties, as well as fend off danger from within,** as the ring works its evil charm on him and those around him.

The film's problem comes in cramming so much story into even three hours, and from the moment Liv Tyler's elf princess pops up, the pacing seems slightly   15 off – skipping from one breathless chase scene to the next. Also, while the scenes with the rank, fearsome orcs are superbly realised, Jackson finds representing the spirit of good much more difficult – soft-focus photography and bright light are his unsatisfactory ploys. This is all the more disappointing when compared to the other groundbreaking effects work on display.   20

The casting, however, could not have been better. **Wood is perfect as Frodo, the vulnerable, slightly weedy central figure whose resolve will no doubt grow with the films, while Billy Boyd and Sean Astin nearly steal the picture as the accident prone comic relief.** Nearly, but not quite. That is left to Viggo Mortensen as mysterious warrior Aragorn.   25

Brooding, intense, and handy with a blade, Mortensen is the film's greatest strength – Han Solo to Wood's Luke Skywalker. The 'Star Wars' comparison is an apt one, for if the next installment, 'The Two Towers', can build on this hugely impressive franchise starter, George Lucas better look to his laurels.

Review by Nev Pierce on *www.bbc.co.uk*, 11 December 2001
Nev Pierce is the editor of *Total Film* magazine and a freelance contributor to the BBC.

> ●●● EXERCISE 4
>
> Who might read this review?
>
> Do you think this is a balanced review? Can you find positive and negative comments about the film?
>
> Do you agree with Nev Pierce's evaluation?

[?] Questions

1 Why do you think the writer begins his review with a list of adjectives?

2 What is meant by the phrase 'least screen-worthy volume'? (lines 3–4)

3 Write down two words or phrases that suggest the writer enjoyed the first hour of the film.

4 Explain – using your own words as far as possible – Nev Pierce's main criticisms of the film.

5 What does the critic mean when he suggests that Boyd and Astin 'nearly steal the picture'? (line 23)

6 Do you think this is a balanced review? Support your answer with evidence from the passage.

7 Why should George Lucas, the Star Wars director and producer, be worried about this film, according to Nev Pierce?

[↔] Extension

8 If you have seen *The Fellowship of the Ring* yourself, write your own review of it in no more than 300 words. If you have not seen the film (or you saw it some time ago and have forgotten much of it) then review a different film that you have watched recently.

9 Do you like film adaptations of well-known books? Do you think they spoil the original, written stories, or do they enhance them and make them even more popular? Write a paragraph in which you share your views. You may refer to books you have read and films you have seen.

10 Write a literary review for a book you have read recently. Try to choose one that has not been made into a film, yet!

[📖] Wider Reading

11 Check out Nev Pierce's reviews of the next two films in the Lord of the Rings trilogy at www.bbc.co.uk/films/lordoftherings
Do you agree with his comments? Would you give each film a different rating? Read the reviews and discuss your responses to them with a partner.

12 You will find a wide selection of reviews of children's books at the following websites:
www.wordpool.co.uk
www.readingmatters.co.uk
Read reviews of books you are familiar with and see if you agree with the critics. Then write your own reviews of similar books.
Remember: there is no right or wrong view – it is a matter of opinion.

UNIT 2
STUDYING POETRY

INTRODUCTION

The poet William Wordsworth (1770–1850) once defined poetry as 'emotion recollected in tranquillity'. This is a good place to begin, for poetry is very much to do with emotions – those of the poet and of the reader too.

Poetry allows us to revisit places we have been or situations we have experienced and recall the emotions we felt when we were there – without ever leaving the comfort of our own homes. We can imagine landscapes, feel the wind in our hair and even smell the breeze, if we try.

A well-written poem can *affect* us. It can inspire our imagination, stimulate our senses and change the way we feel.

Poetry conjures up images in our head, reminding us of similar places we may have once travelled to or experiences we might have once had. But a poem can do more than stir our memory: it can actually affect our *mood*.

When studying poems – and answering questions about them in examinations – we are required to examine how poets create such dramatic effects using nothing but words.

In order to understand this, it is important to look at the poetry techniques they use.

● ● ● EXERCISE 1

Read the following lines from a poem by William Wordsworth:

> There was a roaring in the wind all
>   night;
> The rain came heavily and fell in floods;
> But now the sun is rising calm and
>   bright;
> The birds are singing in the distant
>   woods;
> Over his own sweet voice the Stock-
>   dove broods;
> The Jay makes answer as the Magpie
>   chatters;
> And all the air is filled with pleasant
>   noise of waters.

From 'Resolution and Independence' in *Selected Poems* (Bloomsbury, 1905)

As you were reading the lines, what could you see in your mind's eye? Describe to a partner the images that drifted through your head as you read the words. Focus on your senses when describing your response.

POETRY TECHNIQUES

Imagery

Imagery is descriptive language used in stories and poems to create pictures in the reader's head. It may be **literal**, which means it can be taken literally to mean what it says – e.g. *the sun shone brightly* – or it can be **figurative**, which means it is not intended to be taken literally, but rather as a way of creating dramatic effect – e.g. *the golden gem glistened in the sky*.

Figurative imagery uses **similes** and **metaphors**.

Simile: a phrase that compares two similar things, by using the words *like* or *as*. E.g. *He was caught like a mouse in a trap; Her head felt like glass.*

Metaphor: a word or phrase that should not be taken literally but is used to create a dramatic effect. Metaphors go further than similes: rather than saying the teacher is like a raging bull, a metaphor will say that the teacher *is* a raging bull.

Personification is a special type of metaphor. In personification, human characteristics are carried over to non-human things like animals, trees, houses and rocks, in order to create dramatic effect, e.g. *The trees arched their backs and spread their fingers; The great cliff surveyed its kingdom below.*

As you read through the different poems in this unit, look out for the way imagery has been used to create an impact on the reader.

Sound

Another way of making an impact on readers is by selecting words for their **sound** as well as their meaning. This is what distinguishes poetry from other forms of writing; poems need to be read aloud, so their words can be rolled around in the mouth and enjoyed for the sounds they make.

Alliteration is a popular technique that uses the sounds of words. If we place words together that begin with the same sound, we can create an appealing effect, e.g. *The forest's ferny floor* (Walter de la Mare).

●●● EXERCISE 2

Look again at the lines from Wordsworth's poem in Exercise 1. Can you invent some new similes and metaphors of your own to describe the power and effects of strong winds and heavy rain? Working with a partner, make a list of interesting examples.

Remember: the best similes and metaphors are fresh and exciting. Try to avoid phrases that you have heard too many times before, like *it was raining cats and dogs*, or *the wind howled*.

●●● EXERCISE 3

Can you think of some other alliterative phrases that sound appealing?

Write down some new examples of your own that make use of matching sounds in this way. Share them with your class.

Onomatopoeia is another poetic technique of selecting words especially for their sound. Think of *splash* or *whiz* or *bang*. In each case, the meaning and the sound of the word are the same. Onomatopoeic words can bring excitement to a poem, making the imagery more vivid for the reader.

● ● ● ● EXERCISE 4

Make a list of as many onomatopoeic words as you can. Then write a sentence for each one.

Share your work with the class. Are some words more popular than others?

Rhyme and rhythm

When studying poetry, we might also consider the rhyme and rhythm of each poem, and the way they contribute to the overall impact on the reader.

There are many different rhyming schemes you will see in use. Here are some common ones. See if you can identify the patterns being used.

---

from The Eagle   *Lord Tennyson*

He clasps the crag with crooked hands;
Close to the sun in lonely lands,
Ring'd with the azure sun, he stands.

From *The Dragon Book of Verse*
(Oxford University Press, 1997)

---

from Please Mrs Butler
Alan Ahlberg

Please Mrs Butler
This boy Derek Drew
Keeps copying my work, Miss.
What shall I do?

From *Please Mrs Butler* (Puffin, 1984)

---

from Magpies   *Judith Wright*

Along the road the magpies walk
with hands in pockets, left and right.
They tilt their heads, and stroll and talk.
In their well-fitted black and white

From *The Puffin Book of Twentieth-Century Children's Verse* ed. Brian Patten (Puffin, 1991)

---

from Baby Song   *Thom Gunn*

From the private ease of Mother's womb
I fall into the lighted room.

Why don't they simply put me back
Where it is warm and wet and black?

But one thing follows on another.
Things were different inside Mother.

From *Collected Poems* (Faber and Faber, 1993)

---

from Bags of Meat   *Thomas Hardy*

'Here's a fine bag of meat,'
Says the master-auctioneer,
As the timid, quivering steer,
Starting a couple of feet
At the prod of a drover's stick,
And trotting lightly and quick,
A ticket stuck on his rump,
Enters with a bewildered jump.

From *The Battle Bag* ed. Seamus Heaney & Ted Hughes (Faber and Faber, 1982)

Do you notice the different patterns being used in the examples? How can you describe them? Alternate lines, perhaps? Or rhyming couplets?

A short and easy way to measure and record rhyming patterns is by using the alphabet. Every new rhyming sound that appears at the end of each line in a poem is represented by a new letter of the alphabet. If the rhyming sound has already been used (i.e. it rhymes with a previous line) then the same corresponding letter will be used again.

For example:

In *Magpies*, the rhyming sounds at the end of each line combine to form the following rhyming pattern:

..... walk — *a*

..... right — *b*

..... talk — *a*

..... white — *b*

So this excerpt from *Magpies* follows what we call an '*a*, *b*, *a*, *b*' rhyming scheme.

> ●●● EXERCISE 5
>
> See if you can identify the rhyming schemes of the other poems and excerpts featured on the previous page. Use the alphabet system to measure and record the patterns.

There are, of course, many poems that do not use a rhyming scheme at all. These are written in **Blank Verse**. During this unit, you will encounter poems with different rhyming schemes, and some with none at all.

As well as rhyme, poets may also consider the **rhythm** of the language they are using. When words and phrases are placed together – and then read aloud – a rhythmic pattern may sometimes emerge, and this can often make the reading of poetry more enjoyable.

Look at the following extracts, each taken from a very famous poem.

---

from The Night Mail   *W.H. Auden*

This is the Night Mail crossing the Border,
Bringing the cheque and the postal order,

Letters for the rich, letters for the poor,
The shop at the corner and the girl next door.

From *As I Walked Out One Evening*
(Faber and Faber, 1995)

---

from Skimbleshanks:
The Railway Cat   *T. S. Eliot*

There's a whisper down the line at 11.39
When the Night Mail's ready to depart,
Saying 'Skimble where is Skimble has he gone to hunt the thimble?
We must find him or the train can't start.'

From *Old Possum's Book of Practical Cats*
(Faber and Faber, 1939)

Can you feel the rhythmic patterns in these poems? It is often better to read these kinds of poems out loud and quite quickly, in order to really feel the rhythm coming through. (In both these examples, the rhythm mimics the sound of a passing train).

The rhythm of a poem is called the **metre**, or metric structure. The metre of a poem is measured in **feet**. A foot is made up of two or more syllables placed together. There are special names for different metric feet, including *iamb*, *trochee* and *spondee*.

Well-used metric patterns have special names too, like **pentameter** (five feet), or **trimeter** (three feet).

For now, it is enough to be aware of a poem's metre, and how a poet may have selected certain words for their rhythm as well as their meaning.

Remember: when studying poetry, the sound of words is as important as the meaning!

Atmosphere, tone and mood

Poetry can create **atmospheres**. Through the careful selection of words, poets can conjure up warm, cosy feelings that may comfort us, or they can create a cold, inhospitable atmosphere, which leaves us feeling fearful or unsettled in some way. Just like in real life, atmospheres can affect our **mood** – and this mood can alter, even within the same poem, when poets create different pictures in the reader's mind.

Imagine you are thinking of painting a picture, or taking a photograph. You will probably need to think about colours, textures, light and shadows, and so on. Likewise, in poetry, poets can alter the **tone** of a poem, by using dark, heavy sounding words or quick, bouncy phrases that lift one's spirits. Similarly, poems can have a friendly tone to them, just like a fun piece of music.

The different techniques listed above combine to have an impact on the reader. It is the tone, mood and atmosphere of poetry that makes it such a powerful form of writing, unlike any other.

When studying the poems in this unit, think carefully about the atmospheres they create, and how each poet has used imagery, sound, rhyme and rhythm to alter the tone of a piece and ultimately the effect the mood it creates in us.

THEMES AND STYLES

The types of poems that feature in Common Entrance examinations vary greatly from year to year. There is no predictable pattern. The poems presented in this unit reflect this range. You will see poems that rhyme, others that don't, some that are rich in description, others that are not.

As you study each of the poems, and answer questions on them, think about the **poetry techniques** being used and the ways in which the poems have made an impact on you.

The poems for studying are arranged in themes, comprising:

- landscapes
- people
- school
- seascapes
- cultures
- war
- the environment

Remember: when compared to stories or plays, poems are usually very short compositions, in which every word counts. Poets select each word or phrase for a particular effect – and to understand how they achieve these effects, you need to consider not only the meaning, but the sound, rhythm, tone and mood of the language used.

Discussion

Just like paintings or photographs, poems can capture and record the landscape around us. A mountain view, a castle ruin or a luscious, green valley may be memorised and put down in words for others to appreciate. Poems about the landscape use lots of rich imagery to 'paint a picture' of not only the physical scene, but the mood and atmosphere associated with a particular place.

The British Isles can boast some of the most breathtaking scenery in the world, and for centuries poets have tried to capture in words its changing colours, tones and moods – one of the things that distinguishes us as humans is our ability to respond emotionally to what we see around us. Whether we are relaxing amid the serene valleys and lakes of Cumbria, or tramping across a rain-soaked stretch of Dartmoor, the natural landscape *affects* the way we feel.

Focus

THEMES AND STYLES

- There are as many different themes in landscape poems as there are views for us to see, but common to many is the relationship between man and nature – our place and position in the landscape. From farming and forestry to simple gardening, many of us contribute to the natural sculpture around us, and this is often reflected in poems of this kind. The weather too plays an important part in shaping the landscape and it features frequently in landscape poetry.

- The changeable seasons and different landscapes that surround us are reflected in the range of poetic styles we see on offer in this genre. A landscape poem may offer the reader a slow and peaceful read, inviting them to escape to a Yorkshire Dale or a Welsh Valley, or it may thrill with exciting imagery of bustling city streets and skylines, or even shock and disturb readers with descriptions of landslides, floods and storms.

● ● ● **EXERCISE 1**

Can you remember visiting a place that you found interesting? How did you feel when you were there? Can you describe a snapshot of the view?

Working in small groups, make a list of different landscapes around the country that could make interesting subjects for poems – e.g. a *dark forest*, or a *mountain stream*.

Share your ideas with the rest of the class. Build up a collection of exciting places and attractive views that you could write about in a poem.

POETRY TECHNIQUES

- **Imagery:** As you might expect, imagery plays a very important role in landscape poetry, because it is through adjectives, adverbs, similes and metaphors that poets can build pictures of the places they are describing. Inanimate objects, like trees and rocks, are often given feelings and thoughts through personification.
- **Sound:** The sounds that letters and words make can remind us of the landscape around us. For example, to describe tough, granite rocks, poets might use hard-sounding consonants, like *g-*, *k-* and *d-*. (e.g. a so<u>l</u>i<u>d</u> <u>b</u>lo<u>ck</u>, <u>g</u>uar<u>d</u>ing his <u>king</u>d<u>om</u>). Or softer sounds may be used to describe a stream or spring (e.g. <u>t</u>rickling <u>s</u>o<u>f</u>tly).
- **Rhythm:** The different moods created by the natural landscape can be mirrored in poetry through metric patterns. In other words, to create the feeling of lashing rain, for example, a poet may use syllables and stresses that produce rapid beats, like *pitter-patter, pitter-patter*.
- **Rhyme:** Different rhyming schemes may suit different purposes in landscape poetry. Regular rhymes can excite and amuse readers, cheering their mood and keeping a poem light and frivolous, like a summer's day, or a field of flowers. Rhyming patterns can create a lyrical feel, like a folk song, sung by farmers as they work on the land.

ATMOSPHERE, TONE AND MOOD

When we visit different natural environments, we may often feel different sensations – from relaxed and cheerful, to uncomfortable, unwelcome or even frightened. Poets will seek to recreate these moods in their poems, building atmospheres that *affect* the way we *feel*. A poem about a desolate heath, for example, may cause us to feel unsettled, or even lonely.

POETRY

●●● EXERCISE 2

With a partner, make a list of consonants with hard sounds, like *d* and *k*. Then write down some words with hard consonants to describe the view of a rocky mountain, e.g. *bold and brave...*

Now do the same thing for a gentle stream, running through a forest. This time you will need to select words with soft sounds, like *flowing through ferns...*

Share your ideas with the class.

●●● EXERCISE 3

Have you ever been to a place that you found unwelcoming, or perhaps frightening?

Share your experiences with a partner. Then try to think of some words to describe what these places were like, and how they made you both feel.

Sample

In R.S. Thomas's poem, we learn that a closer look at the beautiful scenery of the Welsh valleys and hills can reveal hidden truths about the landscape.

The Welsh Hill Country
R. S. Thomas

Too far for you to see
The fluke and the foot-rot and the fat maggot
Gnawing the skin from the small bones,
The sheep are gazing at Bwlch-y-Fedwen,
Arranged romantically in the usual manner   5
On a bleak background of bald stone.

Too far for you to see
The moss and the mould on the cold chimneys,
The nettles growing through the cracked doors,
The houses stand empty at Nant-yr-Eira,   10
There are holes in the roofs that are thatched with sunlight,
And the fields are reverting to the bare moor.

Too far, too far to see
The set of his eyes and the slow phthisis
Wasting his frame under the ripped coat,   15
There's a man still farming at Ty'n-y-Fawnog,
Contributing grimly to the accepted pattern,
The embryo music dead in his throat.

From *Collected Poems: 1945–1990* (JM Dent, a division of
The Orion Publishing Group, 1993)

phthisis: a wasting disease, like tuberculosis

●●● EXERCISE 4

How does this poem make you feel? Share your response with a friend.

Discuss the impression you get from the poem about the life of a sheep farmer.

Did you notice how the poet uses hard-sounding words to describe the stony landscape in the opening stanza (or verse)? Look again at line 6 and discuss your findings with a friend.

? Questions

1 Describe the condition of the sheep in the poem.

2 Explain what you think the poet means by the phrase 'Arranged romantically in the usual manner' (line 5).

3 Are the houses in good order at Nant-yr-Eira? Refer closely to the poem in your answer and include quotations, if you can, to support your comments.

4 Explain the following phrase: 'thatched with sunlight' (line 11).

5 Why do you think the poet begins each stanza in the way he does? What effect do you think he might be trying to achieve?

6 To what extent does the weather play a part in this poem? Identify and write down any references to the weather and discuss their impact generally on the poem's mood and atmosphere.

7 Describe in your own words the mood of this poem. Try to support your comments with references to the words of the poem.

↔ Extension

8 Many tourists flock to Wales to enjoy its beautiful scenery. Do you think this poem has a message for them? Explain your answer as fully as you can.

9 Imagine you are the sheep farmer in the poem. Write a diary entry, describing a typical day spent in the remote hills of Ty'n-y-Fawnog. Try to describe the fields, the houses and the livestock that surround you.

10 This poem has a sad feel to it, and yet the Welsh landscape is often considered to be quite beautiful and uplifting. Write your own poem using the same setting, but this time creating a more cheerful, positive atmosphere. You may like to refer to:
   - brighter weather
   - lush green pastures
   - animals: their appearance and behaviour
   - characterful barns and cottages

Wider Reading

11 Read 'Summer Farm' by Norman MacCaig. (You can find it in Andrew Motion's excellent anthology, *Here to Eternity*, published by Faber and Faber in 2001). Compare and contrast the mood and atmosphere of MacCaig's poem with that of R.S. Thomas's 'The Welsh Hill Country'.

12 R.S. Thomas is well known for writing poems about his Welsh homeland, its landscape and its people. See if you can find the following poems by the same writer: 'The Labourer' and 'A Peasant'. Compare the characters in each to the hill-farmer in 'The Welsh Hill Country'.

Discussion

People may well be the most challenging subjects for poets to write about, for we are all complex characters in our own way and often difficult to sum up! Just as a well-painted portrait will capture not only the appearance of a person, but also their character and inner thoughts, so too will a well-written poem.

Close attention to detail often marks out a good portrait poem. Imagine a television camera closing in on an actor's face, revealing the subtle lines and wrinkles, the reflections in their watery eyes and the blemishes on their skin. A poem about a person can present a character in this kind of detail. But it can do more than this: it can tell their story, sharing the daily life that surrounds them and revealing how the subject *really* feels.

Focus

THEMES AND STYLES

- As you might expect, the range of themes in portrait poems varies greatly because we all lead such different and complex lives. But there are some common threads; love, family, friendships, courage, hardship and loneliness are all rich sources of inspiration for poets and they harvest thought-provoking poems that remind us of experiences we may have had in our own lives.
- Just like war poems (see section 2.6), many poems about people draw on 'social realism' – that is to say they describe people's lives in stark reality, not dressed up or romanticised. But this trend is a relatively recent one, and there are plenty of traditional poems that feature more fictional, fantasy characters.

●●● EXERCISE 1

Turn to face a partner. Look closely at their face, then write down a description of what they look like in words. Try to pay close attention to detail (and remember to be flattering or they won't speak to you again!).

●●● EXERCISE 2

Working in small groups, choose a fictional character from a book that you have all read. Write a short character profile together, describing different aspects of your chosen character. You may like to think about:

- appearance
- family background
- likes and dislikes
- thoughts and feelings
- personality

Now think about how you could use this information to write a poem about your character.

POETRY TECHNIQUES

- **Imagery:** Similes and metaphors are often used in portrait poems to emphasise characteristics or features of a person: e.g. *like a mouse, he sat in silence*; *Jane roared at him*; *Tom was all at sea, with no direction.* Just like in stories, characters are brought to life in poems when poets give them real feelings in response to what is happening around them.
- **Sound:** Alliteration and onomatopoeia play their part in poems about people, just like in other types of poetry. Equally, poets will make use of hard and soft consonants to create dramatic effects.
- **Rhythm:** The beat, or 'metre', of a poem can affect the level of suspense within it. For example, if a character in a poem is in distress, or feels frightened perhaps, then you may see shorter lines being used, with stresses that imitate a speeding heart beat. Likewise, slowing down the rhythm of a poem, by using soft sounds, longer words and no apparent syllabic pattern, may convey laziness, tiredness or relaxation.
- **Rhyme:** The rhyming schemes used in portrait poems may help to convey the personality of the character being described. A jolly, friendly person, for example, may be described in light-hearted verse with an appealing and recognisable rhyme.

●●● EXERCISE 3

In pairs, see if you can come up with three suitable similes and metaphors to describe the following fictional characters. Some examples have been included to start you off.

- a bookish lawyer, in a wig and gown (e.g. *a wise old owl*)
- a flamboyant and charismatic actor (e.g. *strutting like a peacock*)
- a very strict teacher (e.g. *a regular sergeant major*)
- an Olympic sprinter (e.g. *he took off like a cheetah*)

Share your ideas with the class.

POETRY

ATMOSPHERE, TONE AND MOOD

The atmosphere, tone and mood of portrait poems will, of course, be affected by the situation in which the character finds him or herself. A whole spectrum of moods may be possible, from joyously optimistic – perhaps celebrating a birth, or a wedding, for example – to sad and melancholy, for a life lost or another life spoiled. In all cases, the poets will try to build empathy in the readers, as they gain insight into the thoughts and feelings of the person being described.

●●● EXERCISE 4

Working with a friend, or in a small group, construct two mind-maps (or spidergrams). On one, write down all the adjectives you can think of to describe an atmosphere that is 'happy'. On the second mind map, write down all the synonyms you can think of for 'sad'.

You could repeat this exercise using other types of poetic atmosphere, for example: *spooky, comical, unfriendly, relaxing, resentful.*

This exercise will help you when you are being asked to describe the atmosphere created in a poem!

Sample

You meet all sorts of people in cities. The men in Stephen Spender's poem leave a lasting impression on the author, as he passes them by.

Unemployed
Stephen Spender

Moving through the silent crowd
Who stand behind dull cigarettes,
These men who idle in the road,
I have the sense of falling light.

They lounge at corners of the street   5
And greet friends with a shrug of shoulder
And turn their empty pockets out,
The cynical gestures of the poor.

Now they've no work, like better men
Who sit at desks and take much pay   10
They sleep long nights and rise at ten
To watch the hours that drain away.

I'm jealous of the weeping hours
They stare through with such hungry eyes
I'm haunted by these images,   15
I'm haunted by their emptiness.

From *Collected Poems: 1928–1985* (Faber and Faber, 1985)

● ● ● ● EXERCISE 5

Discuss the following questions with a friend:

Whom do you think Stephen Spender is talking about here: homeless people, living on the streets; retired workers; or perhaps men who have lost their jobs?

How would you sum up the atmosphere, tone and mood of this poem?

? Questions

1 Write down an alternative word or phrase for *idle* in line 3.

2 In line 4, do you think the poet is referring literally to the day drawing to an end, or could this line have a metaphorical meaning?

3 What clues do you get from the poem about how the men on the street corners feel? Use quotations from the poem to support your answer.

4 How do you react to the phrase 'better men' in line 9? What do you think the poet is trying to suggest here?

5 Do you think the title of this poem is an effective one? Explain your answer as fully as you can.

6 In his poem, Stephen Spender creates an image of people on the edge of society, with no power or influence over what goes on around them. Find two words or phrases from the poem that illustrate this and explain why you have chosen them specifically.

7 Why do you think the poet has chosen to repeat the phrase 'I'm haunted...'? What effect does this repetition have for you, as the reader?

⟷ Extension

8 Do you think the poet has sympathy for the men in the poem or not? Explain your answer as fully as you can, including quotations where appropriate.

9 Comment on the final line of the poem. Is this an effective way of concluding the poem? What does it say to you?

10 Write a similar poem of your own, this time from the point of view of a homeless person living on the streets of a large city. You may like to think about:

- how you spend your days
- your thoughts and feelings about being homeless
- the reactions of the people who pass you by

📖 Wider Reading

11 Compare and contrast the tone of this poem with that of Robert Louis Stevenson's 'The Vagabond' (featured in *The Dragon Book of Verse* published by Oxford University Press in 1977). In the poem, you will find a homeless character who seems thankful for his freedom: 'Wealth I seek not, hope nor love, Nor a friend to know me...'

12 Sir Stephen Harold Spender (1909–1995) was an accomplished poet, literary critic and editor. He enjoyed friendships with many other great poets, including W.H. Auden, W.B. Yeats, T.S. Eliot and Ted Hughes.
Find out more about his life and work by visiting:
www.stephen-spender.org
You may like to read in particular his poem entitled 'In Railway Halls, on Pavements Near the Traffic', which arguably is also about poor people living on the streets of a city.

POETRY

2.3 SCHOOL

Discussion

Almost everyone attends school at some stage in their life. The subject of school is close to everyone's heart, because we can all remember our own educational experiences – good or bad.

Poems about school tap into this rich source of memories that we all have. They tell 'real life' stories with which we can all identify. A good school poem reminds us of our own school days – past or present – and evokes empathy within us, as we remember how we felt when we were in similar circumstances.

When writing about school, poets often recall memories of particular incidents, friendships or other moments that left lasting impressions on them into adulthood.

These memories often last a long time and they can even shape the way we think. This is why school is such a rich subject for poets – it affects the way we all feel in later life.

●●● EXERCISE 1

Working in pairs, or in small groups, think back to some significant experiences at school which you might remember as you grow older: a winning moment at sports day, for example, or a musical concert, or a school play that went wrong!

Share you ideas in class. Did some of you choose similar moments?

Focus

THEMES AND STYLES

- When studying poems about school look out for common themes like friendship, discipline, playtime, lessons and, of course, school dinners! Poets write about these things because they are familiar to all of us and they make a poem more interesting.
- School poems vary in style though – many are often humorous and light-hearted, recalling events and experiences that we all recognise. When recounting their own school days, poets will often use the first person (*I* and *me*) and include personal thoughts and reflections.

●●● EXERCISE 2

With a partner, make a list of evocative words and phrases that you might find in a school poem. List your words under the following themes (some examples are provided):

Friendship	Discipline	Playtime	Lessons
e.g. loyalty	e.g. detention	e.g. daisy chains	e.g. arduous

POETRY TECHNIQUES

- **Imagery:** Descriptive language in school poems often focuses on the setting – the appearance and atmosphere of a classroom, for example – or on school characters: the difficult child, the strict teacher, etc. Similes and metaphors may often be used to give a dramatic impression of a teacher, for example: *the king sat on his throne and surveyed his empire* or *the bear charged into the classroom and growled at us...*
- **Sound:** When considering the sound of words, poets may choose to make use of onomatopoeia to bring their poem to life with the sounds of school, e.g. a school bell ringing, or a buzzer to signal the end of a lesson.
- **Rhyme:** Some school poems will use rhyme to create a child-like atmosphere that reminds us of school experiences. Nursery rhymes for example are associated with nursery school; or rhyming songs may be sung in the playground.

ATMOSPHERE, TONE AND MOOD

- The atmosphere or mood of a school poem will depend upon the event or experience it is recounting. A poet may be describing his or her first kiss in the playground, in which case the atmosphere will be romantic! On the other hand, the theme may be 'my first day at school' and the tone may be more melancholy, thoughtful, or even scary.
- Some school poems will be nostalgic in some way – looking back to happier, carefree days spent in the playground, or on the sports field. The mood will be a relaxing one, celebrating the joys of childhood. Alternatively an author might be looking back regretfully at a misspent youth, wasted lessons or, in the case of the sample on the following page, an unruly class!

●●● EXERCISE 3

Can you think of some onomatopoeic words that you might associate with school life? What sort of sounds do you hear around you each day? Some examples to get you started are:

ring, ring (bell), *thwack!* (cricket bat), *clatter* (cutlery).

Can you think of some more? Share your ideas with a friend.

●●● EXERCISE 4

Working with a partner, think of some interesting similes or metaphors to describe the teachers in your school. (Try not to cause too much offence!)

POETRY

Sample

The last lesson in the afternoon can often drag on, as D.H. Lawrence's poem proves, but it may surprise you to discover who is actually speaking here!

Last Lesson of the Afternoon   *D.H. Lawrence*

When will the bell ring, and end this weariness?

How long have they tugged the leash, and strained apart,

My pack of unruly hounds! I cannot start

Them again on a quarry of knowledge they hate to hunt,

I can haul them and urge them no more.   5

No longer now can I endure the brunt

Of the books that lie out on the desks; a full three-score

Of several insults of blotted pages, and scrawl

Of slovenly work that they have offered me.

I am sick, and what on earth is the good of it all?   10

What good to them or me, I cannot see!

So, shall I take

My last dear fuel of life to heap on my soul

And kindle my will to a flame that shall consume

Their dross of indifference; and take the toll   15

Of their insults in punishment? — I will not! —

I will not waste my soul and my strength for this.

What do I care for all that they do amiss!

What is the point of this teaching of mine, and of this

Learning of theirs? It all goes down the same abyss.   20

What does it matter to me, if they can write

A description of a dog, or if they can't?

What is the point? To us both, it is all my aunt!

And yet I'm supposed to care, with all my might.

I do not, and will not; they won't and they don't; and that's all!   25

I shall keep my strength for myself; they can keep theirs as well.

Why should we beat our heads against the wall

Of each other? I shall sit and wait for the bell.

From *The Complete Poems of D. H. Lawrence*
(Wordsworth Editions, 1994)

quarry: an animal, person or thing being chased or hunted

● ● ● **EXERCISE 5**

Who are the 'unruly hounds' in this poem? Why do you think the poet has chosen to use this metaphor? How effective is it?

Can you identify a rhyming pattern here? Use the alphabet system – learned in the unit introduction, page 32 – to measure and record the rhyming sequence in this poem.

Can you describe the tone and mood of this poem? Is it happy or sad, optimistic or pessimistic? Share your thoughts with a partner. Try to find actual words and phrases that support your views.

❓ Questions

1 From whose viewpoint do you think this poem is written? Try to include quotations from the poem to explain your answer.

2 Why is the narrator unimpressed with the books? What is wrong with them?

3 Sum up, in a sentence or two, and using quotations from the poem, the theme of the third stanza.

4 Give an alternative word that means the same as 'amiss' (line 18).

5 What do you think is meant by the phrase 'It all goes down the same abyss' (line 20)?

6 What effect is created by starting and ending this poem with references to the ringing of a bell? What does it make you think of?

7 What do you think has caused the speaker to feel so despondent? Explain your answer as fully as you can, and with close reference to the poem.

↔ Extension

8 Comment on the author's use of questions in the poem. What effect does this have on the reader's impressions of the speaker and his state of mind?

9 Compare and contrast the tone of the first and last stanzas. How has the speaker's mood altered by the end of the poem?

10 Write your own poem about the same lesson featured in Lawrence's poem, but this time from a pupil's point of view. Will he or she feel the same?

📖 Wider Reading

11 Read 'The Village Schoolmaster' by Oliver Goldsmith. (You can find it in *The Dragon Book of Verse*, published by Oxford University Press in 1977.) Compare and contrast its main character, the schoolmaster, with the teacher featured here in Lawrence's poem.

12 D.H. Lawrence was himself a school teacher before becoming a full-time poet and author. Find out more about his life and work by visiting the following websites:

www.lawrenceseastwood.co.uk

www.spartacus.schoolnet.co.uk/ JlawrenceDH.htm

POETRY

Discussion

The sea has always provided poets with a rich source of inspiration. From tales of pirates and smugglers, voyages of discovery, or famous sea battles, to the simple sound of waves lapping on a shore, sea poetry can stir readers' hearts, inspire minds and soothe senses.

Poets will strive to tap into our romantic notions of what it is like to live and work on the high seas. With clever use of language and literary techniques, a poet will conjure up images, moods and atmospheres that enable us to escape to the coast to experience the pleasures – and the pains – of a seafarer's life.

 ## Focus

THEMES AND STYLES

- There are many different themes explored in sea poems, from tales of courage and hardship, to patriotic verses of loyalty, honour and duty. Other poems may talk of love and loneliness, as sailors are taken away from homes and loved ones. Some sea poems offer more gentle themes of peace and relaxation on tranquil shores.
- The variety of themes offered in sea poems is reflected in the range of styles you will see. Some sea poems may be presented as fast-paced, thrilling story-poems, recounting adventures, battles and shipwrecks, full of suspense and action. Others may adopt a more gentle style, like sea shanties, lullabies and descriptive poems.

●●● EXERCISE 1

In a small group, conduct a 'brainstorm' session in which you write down all the words and phrases that immediately enter your head when you think of the sea. Share these with the class. Think about the sounds they make, as well as the images they conjure up for you.

●●● EXERCISE 2

Do you know any sea stories? Have you read any poems or novels that recount sea adventures?

Share your reading experiences with a partner. Discuss any fictional sea-faring tales you are familiar with. You could begin by sharing what you know about *Treasure Island*!

POETRY TECHNIQUES

- **Imagery:** Literal and figurative description often plays a very important part in a sea poem. Our imagination is often stimulated by rich and colourful descriptions of the ocean, the weather or the seashore. Metaphors – and particularly personification – are often used to bring the sea to life and attribute feelings to it.
- **Sound:** As you might expect, sound often contributes much to sea poetry. Poets will use onomatopoeic or alliterative phrases to simulate the sound of the sea. Look out for those soft consonants and blends, like *s-*, *sh-* and *sw-*.
- **Rhythm:** Poets may use the rhythm of words and phrases to increase the appeal of sea poems, emulating the rising and falling of waves, for example. When syllables are placed together to create high and low stresses (or feet) the rhythmic pattern (metre) can suggest a repetitive and undulating motion.
- **Rhyme:** This is also useful in sea poems, especially when simulating a sea shanty or other traditional song sung on board ship. Rhyming schemes can make sea poems sound more appealing when read aloud, and they can help to create relaxing, lyrical verses.

ATMOSPHERE, TONE AND MOOD

When studying sea poems, consider how poets use language and literary techniques to create different atmospheres and moods. In an epic tale of piracy and smuggling, for example, a writer may try to create an atmosphere that is thrilling and exhilarating. Other poems will have a gentler, more serene mood, as readers are slowly seduced by onomatopoeic sounds and evocative imagery.

EXERCISE 3

Working in pairs or small groups, make a list of alliterative phrases that use soft consonants and blends – the kind you might find in a poem about the sea. Focus particularly on *s-*, *sh-*, *sw-* and *ch-*.

Some examples are: *soft, silky sand*; *swooping and swaying*; *shoals swim in shallow pools.*

EXERCISE 4

Think of a time when you were near – or on – the sea. Did you find it exhilarating? How were you affected by the sights and sounds around you?

What is it about the sea that often seems so appealing to many of us and can affect our mood so easily? Why do we like to visit the coast? Share your thoughts with a friend.

POETRY

🗨 Sample

The following poem, by Wilfrid Gibson, depicts the hardships and dangers encountered on a sea voyage, and the tremendous courage shown by the sailors as they bravely 'sail on' into uncharted waters...

Sail on, sail on! *Wilfrid Gibson*

The day is dying and the steady breeze
Grows wild and gusty, working to a gale;
And through the threshing gloom the farther seas
Flash angrily. Shall we not shorten sail
And make for harbour while we have the light?   5
Sail on, sail on, sail on into the night!

The night is on us with a swoop and roar
That shudders through the ship from truck to keel:
And we may never reach another shore
On those uncharted deeps that surge and reel   10
Beyond the gleam of the last island-light.
Sail on, sail on, sail on into the night!

? Questions

1 Describe using your own words as far as possible the way in which the wind changes as the poem develops.

2 What do you think the word 'threshing' means in this context? (line 3)

3 Write down a word or phrase from the first stanza that suggests the crew might be sailing into a storm.

4 What do you think is meant by the phrase 'Shall we not shorten sail' (line 4)?

5 Have the sailors sailed through these waters before? How can you tell?

6 Do you think the title is an effective one? Give reasons for your answer.

7 Explain how the poet conveys the determination and courage of the sailors through his use of language in the poem.

⟷ Extension

8 How does the poet use the natural elements – e.g. fading daylight and extreme weather conditions – to bring suspense and drama to the poem?

9 Write a similar poem of your own in which you describe an imaginary sea voyage into uncharted waters. You may wish to think about:
- the first person narrative
- references to daylight/night time and weather conditions to create dramatic effect
- ways of conveying the courage of the sailors involved
- a repeated chorus line throughout

10 Write a brief account of this voyage from the viewpoint of one of the sailors on board. You may write your fictional account as another poem, or as a diary or ship's log.

📖 Wider Reading

11 Read other sea poems and compare and contrast them with Wilfred Gibson's composition. Consider the atmosphere, tone and mood of the poems, and the ways in which the poets have used language and literary techniques to create an impact on their readers. Some recommended poems to begin with are 'Cape Horn' by Giles Dixey and 'Sea Fever' by John Masefield.

12 Find out more about the life and work of Wilfred Gibson (1878–1962). You may wish to begin your research by visiting the following websites:

www.warpoets.org/conflicts/greatwar/gibson

www.spartacus.schoolnet.co.uk/
    FWWgibson.htm

POETRY

Discussion

We are fortunate indeed to live in a vibrant and multicultural society that offers a rich variety of traditions, customs and dialects for us to explore. We are also fortunate because poets from a vast range of ethnic backgrounds have chosen to tell their stories and celebrate their cultures through poetry, via the English language.

It is often through the poetry of other cultures that we may get a glimpse of distant homelands, taste the delights of exotic cuisine, smell those rich, wonderful spices, and hear the songs and chants that are embedded in the cultures and religions of others.

But such poetry can, and often does, go beyond glimpses like these. It may share real stories of hardship, suffering, oppression and persecution. When people have struggled to achieve the freedom that we take for granted, they may wish to tell their story, so that others can learn from it. Very often, they do so through the language of poetry.

Focus

THEMES AND STYLES

- There are as many different themes in multicultural poetry as there are different cultures around the world, but some common ones include: faith, family, politics, work, fashion and cuisine. Some poems may draw on writers' own experiences of hardship, oppression and persecution because of their particular race or religion.
- As you might expect, poems from other cultures offer us a rich variety of styles to enjoy. Some may be written in the dialect that is associated with a particular culture or ethnic background, using words, rhythms and rhymes in ways that surprise and delight us. Others may be descriptive story-poems that narrate the experiences of ancestors in distant homelands.

●●● EXERCISE 1

What do you think the word 'culture' actually means? With a friend, or in a small group, discuss your ideas about this word and see if you can come up with a definition.

Write down some key words that help you to describe what it means. Then share these with your class.

●●● EXERCISE 2

How might you sum up your own culture and ethnic background? Do you follow any traditions or customs that have their origins in other countries of the world?

In a small group, share your knowledge and experience of other cultures.

POETRY TECHNIQUES

- **Imagery:** Poets of different cultures will share stories and traditions of their homelands using a range of descriptive language, including similes and metaphors. Look out especially for the use of personification in the description of landscapes and wildlife. Many cultures use metaphor and analogy to bring their own gods closer to our understanding.
- **Sound:** The descriptions of distant homelands, of customs and practices are brought to life through the sounds of poems as much as their meanings. Poets of different cultures select words very carefully for their alliterative or onomatopoeic qualities. Hard and soft consonants can alter the mood of a poem, from celebratory and welcoming, to bittersweet.
- **Rhythm:** From chanting and singing, to drumming, dancing and playing, rhythm can play an important role in the heritage of other cultures, and many poems reflect this. Poets may use the rhythm of words and phrases to simulate song lyrics and chants. Some may even create the impression of sailing or riding on a desert train, for example.
- **Rhyme:** Rhyme can also increase the appeal of a poem, bringing to life the dialect spoken in ways that interest and entertain us. A lyrical poem that rhymes may give us a closer insight into the songs and chants of a new culture.

ATMOSPHERE, TONE AND MOOD

The atmosphere, tone and mood of a poem from another culture will depend upon what the poet has to say. If, for example, he or she is revealing the effects of intolerance or prejudice shown against another culture, then the mood will be a sombre one, and the tone may be bitter. On the other hand, a poem that celebrates the cuisine of another culture, for example, will be light, bouncy and flavoursome.

●●● EXERCISE 3

Working in a pair, choose a country from around the world. Brainstorm all the different words and phrases you can think of that might be associated with the traditions of that country. So for England, you might put: *Tower of London*, *roast beef*, *St George*, *fish and chips*, *Henry VIII*, *the Church of England*, and so on!

Share your chosen words with your class. You may be able to turn them into a 'multicultural' poem.

●●● EXERCISE 4

When does the atmosphere in your classroom or in your playground *change*? When can you detect a change from a happy and settled mood to a nervous or disrupted one? Is it when someone feels hurt or hard done by?

In a small group, discuss what makes a positive, friendly atmosphere in your classroom. Is it to do with *tolerance*?

POETRY

Sample

In his thought-provoking poem, Bought and Sold, *Benjamin Zephaniah questions why some African poets put pen to paper.*

Bought and Sold   *Benjamin Zephaniah*

Smart big awards and prize money

Is killing off black poetry

It's not censors or dictators that are cutting up our art.

The lure of meeting royalty

And touching high society   5

Is damping creativity and eating at our heart.

The ancestors would turn in graves

Those poor black folk that once were slaves would wonder

How our souls were sold

And check our strategies,   10

The empire strikes back and waves

Tamed warriors bow on parades

When they have done what they've been told

They get their OBEs.

From *Too Black, Too Strong* (Bloodaxe Books, 2003)

OBE – Order of the British Empire: an honour awarded by the Queen for hard work and distinguished service

●●● EXERCISE 5

Can you find some words and phrases in this poem that create an impression of African culture and dialect?

Is there a rhyming scheme in use here? Can you measure and record it using the alphabet system? (Refresh your memory by looking back at the introduction to this unit).

Questions

1 Explain in your own words what is killing off 'black poetry', according to Benjamin Zephaniah.

2 Why do you think the poet has used the word 'is' in line 2, rather than 'are' as you might expect?

3 What are 'censors' (line 3)?

4 According to Zephaniah, what are modern poets striving to achieve? Include quotations from the poem to support your answer.

5 What does it mean to say 'ancestors would turn in graves' (line 7)?

6a) Who do you think Zephaniah is referring to when he says 'Tamed warriors' (line 12)?

 b) Why are they bowing? Refer closely to the words of the poem when answering this question.

7 What do you think drives Zephaniah as a poet, if not riches or notoriety? Try to refer to the words of the poem within your answer.

Extension

8 Do you think the poet is impressed by OBEs? Explain your answer as fully as you can, using quotations where appropriate.

9 In a few sentences, comment on the effectiveness of the poem's title.

10 Imagine that Benjamin Zephaniah is invited to a local radio station to share his views on multicultural poetry and particularly poets of African descent. Write a transcript of the radio interview, including some interesting questions and answers. You may like to think about:

● how important it is to Zephaniah to tell the story of his ancestors

● how he regards the British Empire, its awards and honours

● why 'black poetry', as he calls it, may have forgotten its roots

Wider Reading

11 Benjamin Zephaniah is a lively, provocative and passionate poet. Find out more about the life and work of this celebrated writer by visiting the following websites:

www.benjaminzephaniah.com

www.contemporarywriters.com/authors

12 The world of poetry from other cultures is a rich and varied one, spanning so many continents and communities. Here are some highly recommended poets from different cultures; you may know of several others!

Valerie Bloom – www.valbloom.co.uk

James Berry – www.poetryarchive.org

Levi Tafari –
   www.contemporarywriters.com/authors

Debjani Chatterjee –

http://mysite.freeserve.com/
   DebjaniChatterjee

Grace Nichols –

www.contemporarywriters.com/authors

2.6 WAR

Discussion

Not surprisingly war has been a common theme in poems and stories through the ages, since it has the capacity to evoke strong emotions within us. From early tales of valiant knights and marauding warriors to twentieth century stories of deprivation and destruction in wartime trenches, war continues to inspire writers.

The First World War (1914–1918) was named 'the war to end all wars'. It didn't. But what it did do was change the face of war poetry forever. Up until that time, many poets had talked of heroism, of honour, of returning home from battle in a blaze of glory. Yet few soldiers returned in 1918, and those that did had the most horrific stories to tell of death, grief and loss. It was time to reveal the truth about the horrors of war.

The soldiers' stories had to be told. Their courage and sheer heroism still had to be shared, but so too did the horrors that they faced. Readers needed to know what war was *really* like.

●●● **EXERCISE 1**

In pairs, write down some abstract nouns that you might expect to find in a poem about war. Here are some examples to start you off:

courage sacrifice duty camaraderie pain loss

Share your list of words with the class.

◎ Focus

THEMES AND STYLES

- When studying war poetry you will often find similar themes recurring: human bravery, good versus tyranny, camaraderie, loyalty, duty, and so on. The traditional themes of patriotism, victory, glory and honour, which were so prevalent in earlier war poems, can still be found in modern poetry, but they are accompanied by harsh truths about the horrors of war, about pain and suffering and the tragic waste of human life.
- War poems may be written in a style that inspires and rallies troops: strong rhythmic patterns that simulate marching drums and plenty of patriotic language, composed in rhyme. Others may be written in a more stark, blank verse, describing the realities of war.

●●● **EXERCISE 2**

What, for you, is the purpose of war poetry? To describe the bravery of troops? To inspire readers to join up and fight for their country? Or to show readers how bad war can be?

What do you think? Share your views with a partner.

POETRY TECHNIQUES

- **Imagery:** More traditional war poems often use figurative language – similes and metaphors – to rouse patriotic readers and depict arch enemies in dramatic ways, e.g.

  In our heart of hearts believing
  Victory crowns the just,
  And that braggarts must
  Surely bite the dust,

  (From *Men Who March Away (Song of the Soldiers)*
  by Thomas Hardy)

  When war poetry depicts the harsh realities of trench life, however, elaborate metaphors are sometimes replaced with literal descriptions of hardship and suffering.

- **Sound:** Warfare often consists of long periods of silent waiting, followed by sudden bursts of gunfire and bombing, then followed by silence again. Such a pattern may be reflected in war poetry. Battle scenes might be described using ugly, onomatopoeic, hard-sounding words, composed in short lines in quick succession. Other lines may sound softer and slower, simulating long, lonely hours spent in trenches.

- **Rhythm:** When reading war poetry, listen out for rhythmic patterns that imitate the sound of marching drums or gunfire. A poem's metre may contribute to the overall impact that the words have on you as a reader. The rhythm of some patriotic poems can make you feel like putting on a pair of boots and marching!

- **Rhyme:** You will find a vast range of different rhyming schemes in war poetry, and some poems will be written in blank verse. Whatever type of verse you encounter, always think about how, and why, the rhyming scheme contributes to the poem's impact.

> ●●● **EXERCISE 3**
>
> Get into small groups of about three or four. Write down all the onomatopoeic words you can think of that might be associated with warfare. You could begin with: *whiz, crash, thud, clatter...*
>
> Then see if you can turn each word into a more interesting phrase, e.g. *the whiz of a smoke bomb, the crash of glass, an explosive thud, the clatter of gunfire...*

POETRY

ATMOSPHERE, TONE AND MOOD

By now, you will have already learned that the atmosphere, tone and mood of war poems may have altered as a result of the Great War. The exciting, epic tales of valiant soldiers fighting for king and country may still remain, and they are very interesting to read, but so too are the more modern verses that create a very different atmosphere of hopelessness, suffering and loss. Some are even bitter, angry and resentful.

> ●●● EXERCISE 4
>
> Different people hold different views about war. With a friend, imagine you are two young adults who have been 'called up', which means you have received orders to join the army and fight overseas. One of you has been reading stories and poems about epic battles and glorious victories and you are *really* excited about fighting for your country. The other has heard some frightening stories about what can really happen in war, and you do not want to go.
>
> Role-play a short conversation. Then share it with your class.

Sample

In the following poem, by W.B. Yeats, we are reminded of the pointlessness of war.

An Irish Airman Foresees His Death   *W.B. Yeats*

I know that I shall meet my fate
Somewhere among the clouds above;
Those that I fight I do not hate,
Those that I guard I do not love;
My country is Kiltartan Cross,
My countrymen Kiltartan's poor,
No likely end could bring them loss
Or leave them happier than before.
Nor law, nor duty bade me fight,
Nor public men, nor cheering crowds,
A lonely impulse of delight
Drove to this tumult in the clouds;
I balanced all, brought all to mind,
The years to come seemed waste of breath,
A waste of breath the years behind
In balance with this life, this death.

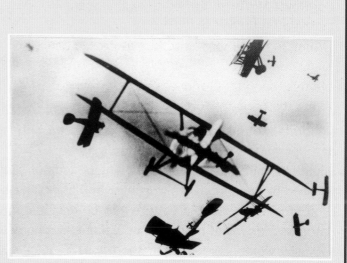

From *First World War Poems*,
ed Andrew Motion
(Faber and Faber, 2003)

●●● EXERCISE 5

Can you describe the tone and mood of this poem? How does it make you feel? Share your responses with a friend.

Do you feel sorry for the character in the poem? How would you feel if you were in his position?

❓ Questions

1 Do you think the Irishman in the poem is aware that he may not survive the war? How can you tell?

2 In which of the three armed forces, Army, Navy or Royal Air Force, do you think this man served?

3 What, in his words, drove him to join up and fight?

4 Is this man afraid of death? Give evidence from the passage to support your answer.

5 Do you think the soldier has enjoyed a fulfilled life until now? Give evidence from the poem to support your answer.

6 What impression do you get of the soldier's own view of war? Explain your answer as fully as you can, and with reference to the words of the poem.

7 Describe the mood of the soldier in this poem.

⬌ Extension

8 In the final line, the poet refers to the word 'balance'. Explain how Yeats conveys the idea of weighing up the odds and balancing one's views throughout the poem. You may like to consider the poet's use of repetition and rhyme in your explanation.

9 Write a letter from the Irishman to his family back home in Kiltartan, in which he shares his thoughts and feelings about where he is, what he is doing, and why.

10 Has the poem altered the way you think about war? Write a paragraph in which you share your own thoughts about the purpose of war.

📖 Wider Reading

11 Explore further the differences in style between war poetry written at the beginning of the First World War and poems that came later. Begin by comparing and contrasting the following: 'Men Who March Away' by Rudyard Kipling and 'Dulce et Decorum Est' by Wilfred Owen.

12 Find out more about war poetry by visiting the following websites:
www.warpoetry.co.uk
www.poetsagainstthewar.org
www.warpoets.org
Use these and other websites to research the life and work of a particular war poet – Wilfred Owen or Siegfried Sassoon, for example. Read some of their work and then try to find out where and how they found inspiration for their poems.

POETRY

POEMS ABOUT THE ENVIRONMENT

Discussion

How we care for the natural environment that surrounds us and sustains us is of great importance – perhaps the most important issue we shall ever face. The damage we are inflicting on our planet, through pollution, deforestation, road-building, house-building and industrial accidents, for example, may be irreversible. So politicians, scientists and environmentalists around the world work hard to change people's attitudes and habits.

And poets play their part too. Poems with a conservation theme can be very effective in reminding readers how precious our planet is. From exotic species, threatened with extinction, to large-scale damage caused by oil spills, there are many topics that will inspire poets to put pen to paper.

●●●● EXERCISE 1

What are we doing to the environment? In what ways are we all damaging it?

Working in small discussion groups, share your views about the environment. Think about how it is being damaged and then consider the ways in which we can all help to save it. These are the issues that you may find in poems about the environment.

Focus

THEMES AND STYLES

- Poems in this genre share a theme of conserving the environment and all that it has to offer. Most will contain a message for readers: look after this beautiful planet and it will look after you. This message may be conveyed through descriptions of precious wildlife or landscapes, which are, in some way, threatened by Man's actions.
- As you might expect, environmental poems come in all shapes and sizes. Some may be long, descriptive poems, intended to remind readers how precious their world is. Others may be short, provocative poems designed to make readers stop and think.

●●●● EXERCISE 2

If you had the opportunity to give one message to the world's population, what would it be?

With a friend, jot down some possible ideas for global messages that might change the way we all think about the environment.

Remember, changing people's attitudes is a very difficult thing to do!

POETRY TECHNIQUES

- **Imagery:** The language of environmental poems will often be rich and 'luscious', reflecting the natural world around us. Adjectives, adverbs, abstract nouns, similes and metaphors all help to paint vivid images of the world. Very often, personification is used to give animals and plants human feelings; perhaps this is the only way some of us will sympathise with them and respect them more!

- **Sound:** This plays an important part in environmental poems. Sharp contrasts can be highlighted between soft, luscious landscapes, rich in nature, and more rugged outlooks, by using hard and soft-sounding words, like *sweet*, *soft* and *plentiful*, as opposed to *dark*, *dull* and *barren*.

- **Rhythm:** All forms of nature beat to a rhythm of some sort. Indeed, it is said that with no movement, there can be no sound – and no life. This is often reflected in environmental poetry, with poets taking special care to create rhythmic patterns that capture the lively sounds of landscapes like rainforests or jungles. Where life is threatened, rhythms will slow down and become less frequent.

- **Rhyme:** To increase the appeal of their work, some environmental poets may use lively rhyming schemes. When verse is written in rhyme it is often easier to remember – like a song – and this is useful if a poet is intending to pass on an important message about conservation.

ATMOSPHERE, TONE AND MOOD

The atmosphere, tone and mood of an environmental poem will depend upon the message the poet is trying to convey. Look out for tones and moods that change slowly throughout the poem, because the writer is showing you what happens when a rich and beautiful landscape is slowly destroyed. The mood may alter from a positive and relaxing one at the beginning to a more urgent and worrying one at the end.

POETRY

● ● ● EXERCISE 3

Working in pairs or small groups, think of a particular landscape – a rainforest or jungle, perhaps. Then write down all the different sounds that you might expect to hear if you were standing in this place.

Think about how you could describe this 'symphony' of sounds in a poem. What words would you use? (You might like to think about alliteration and onomatopoeia.)

● ● ● EXERCISE 4

Think of a time when you were standing in a beautiful part of the country, admiring the view. Did you ever stop to wonder if that view will always be there? This is the job of environmental poets – to prevent us from taking the landscape for granted.

In pairs, choose a particular place of beauty you have visited. In a large table of two columns, describe this place now, in all its beauty, and then describe how it might look with a giant motorway running through it.

Sample

Oil spills can have devastating effects on the life and landscape of our shores – as Brendan Kennelly's poem shows us.

The Hope of Wings   *Brendan Kennelly*

The girl forces the gull's beak open with
A spoon and starts to scrape the oil away.
Rampant the sky's colours, legend and myth
Sustain the attention of those beset by
Traditional hungers, but now I foresee   5
A bird-emptied sky, the world's shores
Hilled with crippled things, the thick black
Smothering oil murdering the hope of wings,
And this girl – she can't be into her teens –
Would, if her working now is a guide,   10
Spend all her years remaking these stunned birds
Littering the sea, dead flops among stones.
She'd give a white-winged creature to the sky
Before black tides destroy mere human words.

From *Familiar Strangers: New & Selected
Poems 1960–2004* by Brendan Kennelly
(Bloodaxe Books, 2004)

●●● EXERCISE 5

In pairs, take turns to read this poem aloud to one another.

Then play a hot-seating game in which each person takes a turn in playing the role of the girl in the poem. The other partner asks the character a series of questions to learn more about the disaster and her reactions to it. You will both need to use your imagination.

Can you detect a rhyming scheme in this poem? How would the atmosphere, tone and mood of the poem change if there was a clear and regular rhyme to it?

? Questions

1 Where do you think this oil has come from? Try to quote from the poem in your answer.

2 What does the word *sustain* mean (line 4)?

3 Rewrite the following phrase in your own words, keeping the same meaning as far as possible: 'now I foresee... the world's shores/ Hilled with crippled things' (lines 5–7).

4 Explain what you think the poet means in the following phrase: 'murdering the hope of wings' (line 8).

5a) How do you respond to the first two lines? Refer to specific words and phrases in the poem when explaining the impact that it has on you.

  b) Why do you think the poet chose to begin his poem in this way?

6 Comment on the poet's choice of title. Is it effective? What do you think it is referring to?

7 Referring closely to significant words and phrases, describe the mood of this poem.

⟷ Extension

8 In lines 5–6 Brendan Kennelly says he can 'foresee/A bird-emptied sky'. Write a few sentences describing how you would feel if the poet's premonitions were to come true.

9 What message does this poem hold for us? Explain your answer as fully as you can, with particular reference to the last two lines.

10 Write a piece of descriptive prose in which you describe the sights, sounds and smells of a stretch of coastline, after an oil spillage.

📖 Wider Reading

11 On the following website, taken from the homepage of the World Wildlife Fund, you will find lots of information about 'wildlife, habitats and threats'. Click on a particular topic, research it, and then write an environmental poem about it:

www.wwf.org.uk/core/wildlife/wildlife.asp

12 The poem featured in this unit is taken from a collection of interesting poems with a conservation theme, edited by Judith Nicholls, called *What on Earth...?*. See if you can obtain a copy from a bookshop or library.
If you thought poems about the environment were a new phenomenon, be sure to read 'The Poplar Field' by William Cowper (1731–1800), which also features in the same collection.

POETRY

UNIT 3
STUDYING PROSE

INTRODUCTION

'Prose' is the name we give to ordinary written (or spoken) language that is composed in sentences and paragraphs, without a specific rhyme or rhythm. Poetry, for example, is not prose. This unit focuses upon a particular type of prose: storytelling.

Storytelling is rather like the mythical art of alchemy – turning base metals into gold. A good storyteller takes ordinary words and phrases, which on their own are worthless, and turns them into something valuable. A well-written story can become very precious, not to mention lucrative for its creator.

Others might see storytellers as sculptors, grouping and shaping words into a whole, which can then be read and appreciated by an audience. The question is: what sort of story will they write?

Story prose is fictional – that is to say it is 'made up' – as opposed to the non-fiction you encountered in Unit 1, which is based on real life. Some stories may actually be based on truth, with real people and places, but most will offer fictional characters, situations and settings, that exist only in the writers' – and the readers' – minds.

During the course of this unit, you will encounter a range of different story genres, including: fantasy and science-fiction; crime; ghost stories; war stories; human interest; and adventures. Each will leave a very different impression upon you. To find out how these differences are created – and to study fictional prose properly – you will need to consider the story techniques that make up the storyteller's craft.

EXERCISE 1

Stories can be grouped into different types or 'genres'. Think of the stories you have read recently. What sort of stories were they?

With a partner, write down some different story genres. You could start with *ghost stories*.

STORY TECHNIQUES
Setting and context

The setting in which a story takes place is an important consideration for authors. For readers to be able to build pictures of characters and imagine the action as it develops, they will need a good description of the 'backdrop' or 'scenery' for the story. Then they can build this imaginary world in their heads, and enjoy revisiting it whenever they dip into the book. A story might be set on the coast, for example, or in the mountains, or perhaps in a new and exciting fantasy world.

When thinking about the setting – or backdrop – to a story, it is important to consider not only where the action takes place, but *when*. An author may decide to write an historical novel, set in a particular period of history, like the Second World War, for example, or may choose to write a science-fiction story set in the future.

When studying the different story genres in this unit, consider where and when the stories are set.

● ● ● EXERCISE 2

Can you remember some of the backdrops to the stories you have read? Could you revisit those imaginary places in your head now?

Describe some of the story settings you have encountered to a friend. Remember to think not only about the 'scenery' but the time too.

Share your findings with the class. Are there any settings that are more popular than others?

We are all affected by the people and places around us, and the era into which we have been born. Fictional characters in stories are no different. The **social** and **historical** contexts for each story help to shape its characters, develop its plot and, ultimately, contribute to the appeal it may hold for readers.

A story set in England in 1940, for example, may be concerned with war and conflict, evacuation, or rationing on the Home Front, and these factors will have an influence over the fictional lives of the characters within it, and the situations they encounter.

Remember: just like real life, stories have a **setting** and a **context**. They cannot exist in thin air without any reference to places, times and the circumstances of the age. When studying fictional prose, observe how authors use the setting and context to build a backdrop against which their story can unfold.

Characters and plot

Sometimes we can become so involved in a story that it seems hard to believe that the characters within it are not real. There are plenty of well-known fictional characters that have become so famous over the years they seem indistinguishable from real celebrities we read about in newspapers and magazines – like Sherlock Holmes, James Bond, or the infamous young Potter!

Getting to know a story character – observing their funny ways, watching their reactions and gaining insights into what they are thinking – can make reading a hugely rewarding activity.

● ● ● EXERCISE 3

Are there some fictional characters you particularly admire? Do you think of the characters in your favourite stories as companions?

Share your thoughts with a friend and then feed back to the rest of the class. Are there some characters that are popular favourites? Can you identify why they are so popular?

Fictional characters are brought to life by authors. The more realistic a character may seem, the more we will identify with him or her and want to find out more about them (and join them on another adventure by buying the sequel!).

When studying fictional prose in class or for an examination, you will need to consider the methods which authors use to bring their characters to life – a process called **characterisation**.

A storywriter may provide readers with rich descriptions of each character, describing their appearance, their personality, their likes and dislikes, and so on. Look for those adjectives, adverbs, similes and metaphors.

At other times, we may learn a lot about a character by observing the way he or she reacts in fictional situations – and the way others react to them. Just like real people, story characters will respond emotionally to what happens around them. Look at how characters act, what they say, and how they feel in response to situations they find themselves in. See how authors share the thoughts and feelings of characters in their stories.

The sequence of events that make up a story is known as the **plot**. The setting for a story may help to make it appealing to readers, and the characters within it may provide company and intrigue, but it is the plot that will engage readers' interest enough to compel them to read on.

When studying fictional prose, look for the ways in which authors piece together the events that take place. Think of the plot as a timeline, moving in one direction, with major events plotted along its route. Some stories – crime fiction, for example – may have quite a complicated plot, with several subplots and tangents leading off from the main storyline.

●●● EXERCISE 4

Getting to know a story character is like making a new friend. But just how well do you know your own friends?

Think of someone you know well who does not attend your school. Find a partner – someone who has never met your friend. Take turns in describing your chosen person to your partner. Think carefully about:

- their appearance
- their family background
- any likes and dislikes they may have
- what they like to do in their spare time
- their personality
- any strong feelings or opinions they may hold

●●● EXERCISE 5

Working with a partner, or in a small group, choose a well-known story and then see if you can present the main events of the plot on a story timeline, moving from left to right.

Share your timeline with the class. Are there any major events you have missed from the plot? Can you identify the most exciting moments in each story?

Language and style

Authors use language in the same way that artists might use paints and brushes (or an alchemist uses base metals!) – to produce original creations, that enthral, intrigue and move us as readers. Though the settings and characters that appear in stories may stand out, it is the way in which authors use language that distinguishes them from one another.

Different story genres call for different language styles, and you will encounter many different examples in the following unit. Crime fiction, for example, is known for its detailed, literal descriptions of characters; fantasy stories may offer rich, figurative imagery, painting colourful images of other worlds; and an action-packed adventure story may dispense with long-winded descriptive paragraphs in favour of fast-paced story narration.

Similarly, fictional prose written many years ago may differ in style and vocabulary from the work of more contemporary authors, writing for today's readers.

You will encounter a range of old and modern prose in this unit. As you work through each excerpt, see if you can identify how story writing has changed over the years. For example, you could begin just by looking for any differences in sentence length.

RANGE OF STORIES

There are many different genres in the world of fiction. This unit offers you a brief glimpse at some of them, including:

- crime fiction
- ghost stories
- fantasy and science-fiction
- war stories
- human interest
- adventures

As you work through the unit, read the prose excerpts offered, attempt the practice questions that have been set and think about the differences between each genre. If you come across a type of story that is new to you, try it out: find the books mentioned and give them a go for yourself. One of the best ways of preparing for any English examination is to broaden your own reading diet. We may all have our favourite types of stories – from crime fiction to fantasy – but, just like exotic food, you never know what else you might enjoy, until you try it!

●●● EXERCISE 6

What kind of writing do you prefer? Do you like to read detailed descriptions of places and people, or do you prefer to get straight into the action of a story?

Share your preferences with a partner.

Discussion

Crime writers are among the best storytellers in the world. A good detective story requires an ingenious plot full of mystery and suspense, rich and varied characters, and, at its heart, a crime that baffles and begs the question 'whodunit'?

Crime fiction is known for its detailed and intricate descriptions of people and places, allowing readers to form their own theories as to what has taken place and who the murderer may be. The stories of Arthur Conan Doyle, Agatha Christie and, more recently, P.D. James and Colin Dexter, continue to engage and enthral readers across the world, making this genre one of the most lucrative – and addictive – of them all. A good crime novel can be very hard to put down.

Crime novels are appealing precisely because they are about ordinary people living everyday lives, but concealing some extraordinary secret full of mystery, revenge and deception. Although a crime novel offers a rich mix of complex characters, an author will work hard to ensure that each one is convincing, and, at first glance, ordinary. Crime writers are illusionists: they present an array of characters to us, challenging us to guess which ones are genuine and which are the deceptions. Very often the truth is not revealed to us until the final page!

EXERCISE 1

Most crime novels will have an identifiable hero whose job it is to flush out the criminal and solve the murder mystery.

Can you think of any famous literary heroes of this genre? Working with a partner, make a list of some famous names and their creators. Then discuss together the kind of characteristics they have in common.

Focus

SETTING AND CONTEXT

- Settings for crime novels can vary greatly, but there are common trends. Many crime stories involve a collection of people in a shared place. This offers a community in which the crime then occurs, throwing up a large number of suspects. Often the physical setting will be an **atmospheric place** like an old hotel, a highland castle, a river cruiser, or even the Orient Express train.
- Some crime novels are set in the past, offering writers – and readers – a context different from today, e.g. Victorian times, the 1920s or wartime. In these cases, writers will have to work especially hard to build an accurate picture of the times, with older cars and no televisions, for example.

- Setting a story in a community – or 'social context' – can create an interesting backdrop, with particular rules and customs that have to be followed (and may hamper the detective's work), like a boarding school or a monastery for example.

CHARACTERS AND PLOT

- Every crime novel will have one or more identifiable **hero**, e.g. a police officer, special agent, or private detective. Often the same hero may be used in further sequels. Such a character will be shrewd, observant and calculating.
- Ironically, these characteristics may be shared by the main **villain** in the story, who may be just as clever and cunning as the detective whose job it is to track him or her down. Crucial to every villain in a crime novel is the art of deception: authors will work hard to disguise the true criminal in 'ordinariness'.
- Crime novels offer a wide variety of other characters for readers to get to know (and add to their list of **suspects**). These may be of different ages, and from various ethnic and social backgrounds or classes – from rich heiresses, to humble hotel porters. Most of these characters, it will be revealed, will have their own motives for committing the crime in question.
- Characters may bring interest to stories, but it is the **plot** that makes readers eager to turn over the page. Crime stories need to have lots of surprises along the way, as their heroes uncover those hidden secrets that fester within the minds of the ordinary people in the story. Plots will be carefully thought out, and may include sub-plots and tangents (or 'red herrings') to be pursued by readers before the real truth is revealed, traditionally in a climactic finale.

●●● EXERCISE 2

Where do you think would make an interesting setting for a crime novel?

Working with a partner, or in a small group, choose a particular setting for an imaginary story. Then make notes on the following:

- the appearance and atmosphere of the place
- the different people (or suspects) you might find there

Share your ideas with the class. Are there some popular types of characters that crop up regularly in crime novels?

●●● EXERCISE 3

Working in pairs, your task is to devise some interesting characters that might appear in a new crime story set on a luxury cruise liner.

An elderly millionaire is murdered on board ship, en route to the Caribbean. You must come up with ten different characters, each of whom has a possible motive of their own for committing the heinous crime.

Make a list of names and next to each one write a small description. You may like to think about:

- their appearance
- their personality
- any connections they may have to the deceased
- any possible motives

LANGUAGE AND STYLE

- The language used in many crime novels is full of **description**, as the people and places involved need to be described in great **detail** for the reader to enjoy solving the mystery for themselves. Some crime stories are reported in a **factual** way – with specific references to times, dates, locations and so on, like a police report for a crime scene.

- Some crime stories may be narrated in the **first person** (like the sample on the following page). In these cases, they may take the form of a diary or series of letters, written by someone directly involved – like an investigating officer, or, as in the following case, an associate or friend.

- Crime stories will often be written in strict **chronological order**, recounting the events that lead up to and then follow the crime committed. Sometimes a crime story may include **flashbacks**, taking readers back to the 'night of the murder' to check a suspect's alibi or test a particular theory.

●●● EXERCISE 4

If someone asked you to account for your own movements during a particular time period yesterday, or last week, could you do so?

With a friend, take turns in explaining where you were, and what you were doing, at various times over the last week, e.g. between 10 and 11am last Saturday, or between 6 and 7:30pm last Tuesday.

Write down key notes, as you would do if you were an investigating officer!

Sample

In the following excerpt from The Adventures of Sherlock Holmes *by Arthur Conan Doyle, the narrator, Dr Watson, meets up again with his old friend Holmes, and finds he has not lost his eye for a good clue.*

One night – it was on the 20th March, 1888 – I was returning from a journey to a patient (for I had now returned to civil practice), when my way led me through
5 Baker Street. As I passed the well-remembered door, which must always be associated in my mind with my wooing, and with the dark incidents of the Study in Scarlet, I was seized with a keen desire to
10 see Holmes again, and to know how he was employing his extraordinary powers. His rooms were brilliantly lit, and, even as I looked up, I saw his tall spare figure pass twice in a dark silhouette against the blind.

15 He was pacing the room swiftly, eagerly, with his head sunk upon his chest, and his hands clasped behind him. To me, who knew his every mood and habit, his attitude and manner told their own story. He was at work again. He had risen out of his drug-created dreams, and was hot upon the scent of some new problem. I rang the bell, and was shown up to the chamber which had formerly been in part my own.

20 His manner was not effusive. It seldom was; but he was glad, I think, to see me. With hardly a word spoken, but with a kindly eye, he waved me to an armchair, threw across his case of cigars, and indicated a spirit case and a gasogene in the corner. Then he stood before the fire, and looked me over in his singular introspective fashion.

'Wedlock suits you,' he remarked. 'I think, Watson, that you have put on seven and a half
25 pounds since I saw you.'

'Seven,' I answered.

'Indeed, I should have thought a little more. Just a trifle more, I fancy, Watson. And in practice again, I observe. You did not tell me that you intended to go into harness.'

'Then, how do you know?'

30 'I see it, I deduce it. How do I know that you have been getting yourself very wet lately, and that you have a most clumsy and careless servant girl?'

'My dear Holmes,' said I, 'this is too much. You would certainly have been burned had you lived a few centuries ago. It is true that I had a country walk on Thursday and came home in a dreadful mess; but, as I have changed my clothes, I can't imagine how you deduced it. As to
35 Mary Jane, she is incorrigible, and my wife has given her notice; but there again I fail to see how you work it out.'

He chuckled to himself and rubbed his long nervous hands together.

40 'It is simplicity itself,' said he; 'my eyes tell me that on the inside of your left shoe, just where the firelight strikes it, the leather is scored by six almost parallel cuts. Obviously they have been caused by someone who has very carelessly scraped round the edges of the sole in order to remove crusted mud from it. Hence, you see, my double deduction that you had been out in vile weather, and that you had a particularly malignant boot-slitting specimen of the London slavey. As to your practice, if a gentleman walks into my rooms smelling of iodoform, with a black mark of nitrate of silver upon his right forefinger, and a bulge on the side of his

45 top hat to show where he has secreted his stethoscope, I must be dull indeed if I do not pronounce him to be an active member of the medical profession.'

I could not help laughing at the ease with which he explained his process of deduction. 'When I hear you give your reasons,' I remarked, 'the thing always appears to me to be so ridiculously simple that I could easily do it myself, though at each successive instance of your

50 reasoning I am baffled, until you explain your process. And yet I believe that my eyes are as good as yours.'

'Quite so,' he answered, lighting a cigarette, and throwing himself down into an armchair. 'You see, but you do not observe. The distinction is clear. For example, you have frequently seen the steps which lead up from the hall to this room.'

55 'Frequently.'

'How often?'

'Well, some hundreds of times.'

'Then how many are there?'

'How many! I don't know.'

60 'Quite so. You have not observed. And yet you have seen. That is just my point. Now, I know that there are seventeen steps because I have both seen and observed.

> From 'A Scandal in Bohemia' in *The Adventures of Sherlock Holmes*
> by Sir Arthur Conan Doyle (Penguin, 1981)

spirit case: another name for a drinks cabinet
gasogene: a device used in Victorian times for making carbonated (fizzy) water
slavey: a hard-worked maidservant

●●●● EXERCISE 5

Find a word or phrase in the passage that indicates it was written in Victorian times.

From your reading of the passage, what sort of characteristics do you think Holmes possesses that make him an ideal detective and hero for a crime novel?

❓ Questions

1 How did Dr Watson know that Holmes was 'at work again'?

2 What is meant by the following metaphor: 'hot upon the scent of some new problem' (line 18)?

3 Find a word or phrase from the passage which tells you that Dr Watson had once lived at the flat in Baker Street.

4 What do you think the word 'effusive' means in line 20?

5 What leads Holmes to the conclusion that married life suits his friend, Dr Watson?

6 Do you think Holmes is pleased to see his old companion? Support your answer with evidence from the passage.

7 According to Holmes, what is the difference between 'seeing' and 'observing'?

↔ Extension

8 In a few sentences, explain in your own words how Holmes is able to reach the 'double deduction' that his companion has recently ventured out in the rain, and has an inefficient maidservant?

9 This passage is written in the first person narrative, from Watson's viewpoint. How does this influence the impression we, as readers, get of the famous detective?

10 Rewrite this passage, this time writing from Holmes's viewpoint. Try to give readers a clearer description of Dr Watson, as his friend sees him.

📖 Wider Reading

11 Read 'A Scandal in Bohemia' and other short stories by Arthur Conan Doyle in *The Adventures of Sherlock Holmes* (Penguin, 1981). As you read each story, think particularly about how the author introduces each character in fine detail by demonstrating Holmes's powers of observation.

12 Compare and contrast the work of Conan Doyle with that of a more recent crime writer, like P.D. James, Colin Dexter or Elizabeth George. Try to identify similarities and differences in the settings, characters, plot and language styles of the different stories you read.

Discussion

What do you think of when you hear the words **ghost story**? What sorts of images enter your head? A dark, winding staircase? Perhaps an eerie forest and the howl of the wind?

Ghost stories capture our imagination. They thrill us and sometimes frighten us. They draw us in to mysterious places and then leave us feeling unsettled but strangely curious...

So how do authors of ghost stories reach out to their readers and change the way they feel? How can just a few words on a page actually affect our emotions? What are the different elements in good ghost stories that combine to create such an impact on the reader?

 ## Focus

SETTING AND CONTEXT

- Ghost stories are often set in **mysterious locations**: unfamiliar places that have an **eerie atmosphere** of some kind, which adds to the feeling of isolation and suspense that we expect from this genre. A ghostly setting will not allow us to feel safe, or comfortable!
- The context for a ghost story will very often include some **injustice**, a wrong that is yet to be righted, or a crime that has not been avenged. There will usually be a reason why the ghost cannot rest in peace but haunts a place, waiting for justice – and this may result in the fictional setting being the subject of superstitious **rumours**, **folktales** and **legends**.

●●●● EXERCISE 1

Working with a partner, write down some of the mysterious places you might expect to find in a good ghost story. For example: *an old castle ruin* or *an abandoned house*.

Then write down some words together that describe how you might feel if you were left alone in such a place. For example, you might feel: *nervous, chilled, alone, vulnerable...*

●●●● EXERCISE 2

Have you ever been to a place that was thought to be haunted? Share stories of places you have visited or folktales you have heard about ghostly haunts.

With a partner, write down some famous haunted buildings and describe the ghosts that are believed to haunt them!

CHARACTERS AND PLOT

- Most good ghost stories will have a **supernatural presence** of some kind – a ghostly apparition that can be seen, or an eerie chill that can be felt in the air. You will also often find innocent characters who play the necessary role of victims for the ghost to haunt. Ghost stories often have 'experts' too – people who have seen or heard the ghost and can validate the folktales that have built up around the place.

- Most ghost stories will begin with an **ordinary event** – a holiday, perhaps, or a camping trip. The reader will be lulled into a pleasing sense of everyday normality. Characters will be happy and free. Then, slowly or sometimes suddenly, this atmosphere will be shaken by some sort of **supernatural event** and, from thereon, readers will share characters' fears until the ghost has been vanquished, or put at peace.

LANGUAGE AND STYLE

- The language used in ghost stories is often **rich** and **descriptive**; look out for adjectives, adverbs, similes and metaphors that tingle the senses and help to create **suspense**.

- Authors of ghost stories often like to vary the length of their sentences, using long **complex** ones, full of description to set the scene, followed by short **simple** sentences to give readers a jolt or build suspense.

- Much of the impact of ghost stories comes from what is left out as well as what is actually written. A reader's imagination is a powerful ally for ghost writers and they will strive to infer frightening situations and scenarios without actually describing them!

> ●●● EXERCISE 3
>
> Can you think of some strange events that might begin to unsettle the characters in a ghost story – nothing too frightening to begin with, just odd! Make a list of some mysterious happenings that could take place. For example: *a door closing, a window rattling, a cold wind blowing in...*

PROSE

Sample

In the following excerpt, which begins David Almond's novel, Kit's Wilderness, *Kit and his friends visit Askew's den, buried deep inside an abandoned coal mine, where they play his mysterious game of Death.*

In Stoneygate there was a wilderness. It was an empty space between the houses and the river, where the ancient pit had been. That's where we played Askew's game, the game called Death. We used to gather at the school's gates after the bell had rung. We stood there whispering and giggling. After five minutes, Bobby Carr told us it was time and he led us through the wilderness to Askew's den, a deep hole dug into the earth with old doors slung across it as an entrance and a roof. The place was hidden from the school and from the houses of Stoneygate by the slope and by the tall grasses growing around it. The wild dog Jax waited for us there. When Jax began to growl, Askew drew one of the doors aside. He looked out at us, checked the faces, called us down.

We stumbled one by one down the crumbling steps. We crouched against the walls. The floor was hard-packed clay. Candles burned in niches in the walls. There was a heap of bones in a corner. Askew told us they were human bones, discovered when he'd dug this place. There was a blackened ditch where a fire burned in winter. The den was lined with dried mud. Askew had carved pictures of us all, of animals, of the dogs and cats we owned, of the wild dog, Jax, of imagined monsters and demons, of the gates of Heaven and the snapping jaws of Hell. He wrote into the walls the names of all of us who'd died in there. My friend Allie Keenan sat across the den from me. The blankness in her eyes said: *You're on your own down here.*

From *Kit's Wilderness* by David Almond
(Hodder Children's Books, 1999)

●●● EXERCISE 4

Based on what you have learned about ghostly settings, do you think Stoneygate is an ideal location for a ghost story?

Do you remember the types of characters often found in ghost stories? Which one would you say John Askew might be?

Think back to the style of language often found in ghost stories – words that tingle the senses and create suspense for the reader. Can you find any such words in this excerpt? Look for interesting adjectives and adverbs particularly.

❓ Questions

1 How is Askew's den hidden from view?

2 Did the children look forward to their trips to see Askew? How can you tell?

3 Read the following sentence from lines 23–24: 'He wrote into the walls the names of all of us who'd died in there.' Based on the evidence available in this excerpt, what do you think this means?

4 Identify and write down the particular features of Askew's den that create an eerie atmosphere for the reader.

5 A good ghost story will always provoke the reader's curiosity. Describe any aspects of the story so far that leave you wanting to know more. Are there any questions you would like answering now that you have read it?

6 The opening sentence is a simple but effective one. Suggest reasons why the author may have chosen to begin his story with this sentence. What effect does it have on the reader?

7 Based on the evidence in the passage, suggest how the children regard Askew. Is he a hero to them?

⟷ Extension

8 Imagine you are Askew, watching the children creep to your den. How do you regard them? Do you find it amusing scaring them in this way? Rewrite the passage from Askew's viewpoint.

9 Plan and write the opening to a ghost story of your own. Like David Almond, begin by describing the story setting. Remember to try to make the reader feel both curious and unsettled by the eerie quality of the place you are describing. Your aim is to make readers want to read on, even though they know a fright may await them!

10 Why do so many of us like ghost stories and films? Why do we like to be frightened? Write a short discursive essay in which you explore some of the reasons why this genre has enjoyed so much success.

📖 Wider Reading

11 For another exciting story opening, read the prologue to *Moondial* by Helen Cresswell (Puffin Books, 1988). Here the author describes the eerie statues and mysterious shapes in the gardens of a great house, at midnight. Notice how the author appeals to the reader's senses throughout the piece.

12 If you enjoyed reading the excerpt from *Kit's Wilderness*, you may wish to find out more about the author and his work by visiting the following websites:
www.davidalmond.com
www.fantasticfiction.co.uk/a/david-almond

PROSE

3.3 FANTASY AND SCIENCE-FICTION

Discussion

Dipping into a good fantasy or science-fiction novel is like journeying to another world, full of weird and wonderful characters, mysterious places and unique possibilities that you could never have imagined.

This genre is a hugely popular one, in which successful books can be turned into movies and may even inspire merchandise – from comics and collectors' annuals to lunch boxes and pencil cases.

The characters and places we discover in fantasy and science-fiction stories can become almost as real as their creators. But why do we love them so?

The word fantasy means fanciful invention or design, created by our imagination. Similarly, science-fiction refers to stories set in the future using imagined technology. To say something is in the realms of fantasy or science-fiction means it is beyond reality, and yet often things that appear in science-fiction stories become real, eventually.

Focus

SETTING AND CONTEXT

- As you might expect, there are **no limits** to the kinds of settings which can form the backdrops to stories in this genre. Readers may be whisked away to anywhere the writer wishes to take them – other worlds and universes, the past or the future, reality or dreams. What many stories have in common is their 'other worldliness' – the presence of another place or time that is distant from the here and now.
- The contexts for fantasy and science-fiction novels often include some sort of **quest** or **challenge** that the hero or heroine must fulfil – like the search for a magical sword, or the slaying of a dragon.

● ● ● EXERCISE 1

Can you think of some well-known characters from fantasy or science-fiction stories? It is easy to forget that they are not actually real.

With a partner, list all the fictional characters you can think of from this genre, and then discuss their characteristics and what makes them so special.

● ● ● EXERCISE 2

Work in a group of three or four. Focus on a fantasy or science-fiction novel that you are all familiar with. Then consider together the different settings for the story. Is it based in this world or another? Is it set in the past, present or future?

Then choose other stories and discuss their settings. Can you find any similarities across the different books? Do some fantasy worlds remind you of others?

CHARACTERS AND PLOT

- Just as the range of settings and contexts for stories of this kind is limitless, so too are the casts of characters. From aliens and UFOs to trolls, gorgons and unicorns, one can encounter anything or anyone in a fantasy or science-fiction story. However, in order to make these other-worldly characters convincing, authors will work hard to describe them as vividly as possible. Look out for powerful adjectives, personifications, similes and metaphors in fantasy imagery.

- Many fantasy characters possess **supernatural powers** or gifts, such as telepathy, as in John Wyndham's *Crysalids*, or even metamorphosis, as in David Eddings' *Belgariad* characters and Philip Pullman's 'dæmons'.

- Stories in this genre often star a principal **hero** or **heroine**, whose task it is to fulfil the necessary goal or quest upon which the plot is based. Sometimes the heroes may be 'ordinary' humans, surrounded by aliens, ogres or space-age villains!

LANGUAGE AND STYLE

- The fantasy or futuristic worlds in which these stories are set will often bring strange **new names** and **terms** that readers must grapple with. This is all part of the authors' attempts to establish convincing and appealing worlds into which we can escape.

- Some stories in this genre may be written in a lively, quirky narrative – 'wacky' you might say, like Terry Pratchett's *Discworld* stories, Robert Rankin's *Brentford Trilogy*, or the infamous Harry Potter novels. Others, like Phillip Pullman's *His Dark Materials* may introduce readers to more serious and thought-provoking issues concealed within their fantasy settings. Other writers, like George Orwell, create futuristic scenarios that often become eerily accurate a generation later (for example, his famous novel, *1984*).

●●● EXERCISE 3

Of all the fantasy or science-fiction heroes you know, which one do you favour the most? Which character would you most like to be similar to? Discuss your opinions with a partner.

Then consider together the monsters and villains you have encountered in fantasy novels. Which one left the greatest impact on you, and why?

PROSE

Sample

Maggie Pearson's Shadow of the Beast *is a unique fantasy story: teenager Troy is left in a dream-like state after a serious car accident. In his imagination, he returns to the world of myths and legends, believing he is Wiglaf, a Saxon peasant.*

All the boy knew was that he was afraid.

Afraid of what?

A thing without a name.

5 Afraid of every passing shadow, the screech owl's cry, the fox's bark and the pitter-pattering of tiny feet among the undergrowth.

10 At night when they lay down to sleep, fear gnawed at his insides worse than any hunger.

In the morning,

15 breaking camp, setting off again while the world was still licking itself into shape out of the grey mists of dawn, fear dogged his footsteps, closer than his own shadow. Fear peering wide-eyed over his shoulder at the greater fear that lay ahead.

How long had they been travelling? Days? Weeks? He couldn't remember a time before.

20 'Where are we going?'

'That's for me to know,' the blind man said, 'and for you to find out!' He gave a sudden bark of laughter which sent the forest birds into a fluttering panic. The boy found himself unexpectedly alone as the path they were following took a twist around a bramble thicket. He hitched up the bundle on his back, the blankets, the cooking pot and tripod, the harp and the

25 ceremonial feathered cloak, and trotted the next few steps to catch up.

'Why do I have to carry everything?' he grumbled. 'Why can't you lend a hand?'

'Because I am a Bard of the Silver Branch and you are a boy of no account that I found crying by the roadside.'

'Huh!' The bedroll was morphing into a snake, trying to squirm out from under his arm, and

30 the harp had turned affectionate, its strings nibbling at his left ear. 'And what did your last slave die of?' the boy muttered mutinously.

'Of a curse!' the man spat back.

'Pull the other one! People don't die of a curse!'

'Depends who's doing the cursing.'

35 'Oh don't tell me. Let me guess.'

'Always complaining, he was. Thought I'd give him something to complain about, like a plague of boils. Rather overdid it, I'm afraid. He was called Wiglaf, too.'

Through gritted teeth the boy muttered to himself (not that he believed a word of the stuff about a curse, but still you can't be too careful), 'My name is *not* Wiglaf'.

40 'Didn't say his name *was* Wiglaf. *Called* Wiglaf, that's what I said.'

Sunlight filtered green by the forest leaves leached the colour from their faces till they looked like ghosts. Like ghosts they moved through the moist, misty marshes, where men in flat-bottomed boats were slowly, rhythmically gathering reeds, or else sat motionless, eel-spear at the ready, never once lifting their heads to see the two of them pass by.

45 Following a blind man through the marshes, where a single false step — He must be mad. 'How do you know the right way to go?'

'I can hear it! I can smell it! Come on, Wiglaf!'

I am not Wiglaf. Wiglaf is Not – My – Name! What kind of a name was Wiglaf? Short-arsed and thick as cold porridge, with a sad haircut. Whereas he was.... his name was.... *OK, then,*
50 *call me Wiglaf, see if I care!* He hitched up the bedroll again and slung the cooking pot and trivet either side of his shoulder in an effort to stop their ceaseless clank-clank-clanking.

From *Shadow of the Beast* by Maggie Pearson
(Hodder Children's Books, 2002)
Reproduced by permission of Hodder and Stoughton Limited.

● ● ● EXERCISE 4

With a partner, read the passage again and look for any references to the place in which this part of the story is set. Is it an interesting location?

Does it enhance the reader's enjoyment in any way? Does it increase the dramatic effect of the opening chapter?

PROSE

Questions

1   Replace the following metaphor with one of your own, keeping the same meaning and effect: 'fear gnawed at his insides' (lines 11–12).

2   What do you think the author means when he says the boy's bedroll was 'morphing into a snake' (line 29)?

3   What does the word 'mutinously' mean in line 31?

4   Explain briefly what a curse is.

5   Why did the Bard place his last slave under a curse?

6   'Through gritted teeth' (line 38) usually means trying to hide what you are thinking. Why do you think the boy might be doing this here?

7   The words 'fear' and 'afraid' are repeated several times throughout the passage. What do you think the author was trying to achieve through this use of repetition?

8   This excerpt forms the beginning of Maggie Pearson's novel. Do you think it is an effective story opening? Explain your views as fully as you can, with reference to the text, its layout and the dramatic effects it creates.

Extension

9   Write the first page of an imaginary fantasy story of your own, in which a hero or heroine finds him or herself in another world. You will need to think about:
   ● the landscape
   ● other fantasy characters
   ● the reactions of the hero/heroine
   ● the challenge or quest to be faced
   Try to begin your piece in a punchy and exciting way that grabs readers' attention and makes them curious enough to want to read on!

10   Write a continuation of this story, developing the plot in any way you think is appropriate. Where are the characters heading? Who, or what, is the 'Bard of the Silver Branch'?

Wider Reading

11   Read the full version of Maggie Pearson's *Shadow of the Beast*. Then see if you can find out more about the legendary Anglo-Saxon poem, 'Beowulf'. You can find lots of information on either, or both, at the following:
   http://en.wikipedia.org/wiki/Beowulf
   www.lone-star.net/literature/beowulf/
      beowulf.html

12   Did you know there is a magazine devoted to fantasy and science fiction? You can find out more information about it by visiting
   www.sfsite.com/fsf
   You can also join in discussions, read and write fantasy book reviews and see interviews with fantasy and science-fiction writers at
   www.sfsite.com

Discussion

You will have seen in Unit 2 how the subject of war can inspire poets to put pen to paper, and the same can be said for storywriters. People need to know the realities of war – what it does to the lives and the landscapes that it touches – and authors will work hard to create stories that tell of the heroism and the sacrifices made when wars are waged and lives are changed forever.

War stories may involve soldiers on the front line, while others may describe life for families and civilians back home, as they experience rationing, evacuation and perhaps even bombardment. Writing a war story requires a lot of research: authors will often travel to old battle grounds, chat to locals, research records and interview former soldiers, to get the setting and context right for their story.

Focus

SETTING AND CONTEXT

- The settings for war stories will often be divided into two sorts of locations – the **battlefield** and the **Home Front**. Both settings offer authors a rich source of stories about the courage, camaraderie, hardship and suffering of soldiers in action, and civilians back home.
- Wars have been waged in so many nations around the world, and this is reflected in the range of countries featured in war stories. From the battlefields of Northern France, to the caves of Afghanistan, the settings of real wars and conflicts often feature in stories.
- The contexts for war stories will usually be the **real wars** or **conflicts** they are describing, e.g. the Second World War (1939–1945) or the Falklands War (1982). Authors may choose to focus on specific aspects or effects of war, particular **war heroes**, or **individual battles** fought in specific locations.

●●● EXERCISE 1

Working in pairs, share your thoughts about how wars can affect the everyday lives of civilians as well as soldiers. What sort of events and situations might an author of a war story choose to write about?

●●● EXERCISE 2

Can you think of some examples of real locations for war stories? Where have wars occurred around the world?

Share your thoughts with a friend and then offer feedback to your class.

Once you have made a list together of some settings, see if you can think of some actual stories that have been written using each location. Some examples to start you off are:

- *Only a Matter of Time: A story from Kosovo* by Stewart Ross (Hodder Wayland, 2001) – Kosovo, Balkan War
- *Waiting for Anya* by Michael Morpurgo (Mammoth, 2001) – Pyrenees, France/ Spain, Second World War
- *Private Peaceful* by Michael Morpurgo (HarperCollins Children's Books, 2004) – Northern France, First World War
- *Toro! Toro!* by Michael Morpurgo and Michael Foreman (Collins, 2002) – Spanish Civil War
- *Gulf* by Robert Swindell (Heinemann Educational Publishers, 1994) – Iraq, Gulf War

CHARACTERS AND PLOT

- When reading and studying war stories, you will find a rich variety of different characters offered. As you might expect, the individual lives of **ordinary soldiers** are often described in detail, and their accounts can be especially moving. Most important, perhaps, is that the characters will be **realistic** – in other words they will have weaknesses as well as strengths, fear as well as courage. **Heroes** and **heroines** will emerge, and their leadership skills will be tested in difficult circumstances.

- The plot for a war story may follow the course of **events** of a real war that actually took place. What is interesting is the way in which national, or even global events have an impact on the lives of **individuals**, and this factor will help authors plan their story plots. So, for example, a war story may show what happened to one family when evacuation plans were put into effect and rationing was introduced during the Second World War.

LANGUAGE AND STYLE

- Many war stories will include lots of **descriptive prose**, describing the different war-torn locations and the impact upon the lives of characters.

- Authors will often seek to share the **thoughts** and **feelings** of their characters, as they face the hardship and suffering of war. This may be done through the third person (*he felt anxious*) or the first person narrative (*I was sent away*).

- Many, though not all, war stories are written in **chronological order** – like a diary or series of letters perhaps, recounting the events and battles, from one person's viewpoint.

- Just like the war poetry featured in Unit 2, war stories may be written in a **traditional language** that stirs **patriotic feelings** and celebrates Man's courage in 'conquering evil'. On the other hand, some modern texts may offer **'realism'** – the style of writing that depicts the very harsh realities of trench life or living through the Blitz, for example.

●●● EXERCISE 3

Can you think of any well-known heroes or heroines from war stories? They may be real or fictional characters.

Share your ideas in groups of about four or five. Make a list of names. Then discuss what you know about the characteristics of each one.

Some characters to start you off are:

William Beech (from *Goodnight Mister Tom*)

Anne Frank (from *The Diary of Anne Frank*)

Jan (from *The Silver Sword*)

●●● EXERCISE 4

Working in small groups, have a go at constructing your own story plot for an imaginary war story, centred on the life of a young girl or boy evacuated to the countryside during the Second World War.

How will the story unfold? What sort of things will happen to her?

Draw a story timeline and plot different story events along it. You could begin with an announcement of the Government's Evacuation Plan.

Sample

In the following passage, from Theresa Breslin's Remembrance, *we are offered a fascinating account of the thoughts and fears of one young soldier caught up in a vast and terrifying war.*

John Malcolm stood with his fellow soldiers waiting for the signal to go forward. The trenches were full, crushed with the dense pack of men brought up from the rear in readiness for the dawn attack. In front of his battalion were the Royal Inniskilling Fusiliers who 5 were going in as the first wave, and on their right to the rear the men of the Essex's who were to follow after. John Malcolm knew that along mile upon mile of the Front, regiment after regiment of the Army was in a long line ready to engage. They had been told 10 that history would be made today, and he was aware of his own place here with men from Newfoundland and South Africa, from India and Australia and New Zealand, men from Tyneside, Northumbria and Wales. His exhilaration at being part of it ran through 15 his whole being, his mind fired with the words the Corps Commander had addressed to them before the night march from the wood at Acheux. The sense of dislocation that he had experienced on his first tour of duty in the trenches was gone. To begin with, 20 walking in these deep angular fissures of the earth, with the only fixed constant being the narrow running strip of sky above, had made him feel at once remote and insignificant, yet at the same time as if at any moment he could be plucked out and up into the cosmos. All that had now dissipated. This morning he was clearly fixed in time and space, with a deep sense of identity and purpose. He stood with the absolute firmness 25 of spirit that comes with certitude of resolve, his heart singing with confidence.

The bombardment of the previous week meant that there could be little left of the German defences, and they had just heard the sappers' huge mine going off to the north at Hawthorn Redoubt. The Captain's eye was on his watch as the minutes ticked towards 7.30 a.m. As soon as they'd given enough time for the dust to settle, they'd get out and walk forward to mop up 30 any pockets of resistance.

Beside him Eddie Kane swallowed in nervous excitement. 'We're really here! I can hardly believe it. Think of what we're going to tell them when we get back home!'

The whistles for his battalion blew, and laden with his full pack, John Malcolm clambered along the trench line and out through the path marked in their own wire. He struggled to his 35 feet, gripped his rifle firmly with both hands, and walked steadily into the rising sun.

From *Remembrance* by Theresa Breslin (Doubleday, 2003)
Reprinted by permission of The Random House Group Ltd
© Theresa Breslin 2002

PROSE

EXERCISE 5

Do you think Theresa Breslin has painted an accurate picture of trench life here? Is it realistic? How has she achieved such realism?

How do you regard John and Eddie? Do you feel sorry for them? Do you admire them?

Share your thoughts and feelings with a partner.

? Questions

1. Why were there so many men in the trenches at this time?

2. Based on the evidence available in the passage, what do you think was the purpose of the Corp Commander's speech before the march from Acheux?

3. What do you think is meant by the phrase 'sense of dislocation' (lines 18–19)?

4. How had John Malcolm first felt upon arriving in the trenches?

5. Rephrase the following sentence, keeping the same sort of meaning: 'at any moment he could be plucked out and up into the cosmos' (lines 23–24).

6. What does 'dissipated' mean in line 24?

7. In war, soldiers have to battle against their emotions as well as their enemy. Comment on this phrase, supporting your view with evidence from this passage.

⬌ Extension

8. John Malcolm's fellow soldier, Eddie Kane, seems excited to be seeing action overseas.
   a) Do you think many of the men might have felt this way?
   b) How – and why – might these feelings have gradually changed as the men spent more time in the trenches?

9. Explain, with close reference to the passage, how the author manages to convey the human side of war, with its worries, fears and challenges.

10. Continue this piece of prose in whichever way you think is appropriate. You will need to think about:
    - how John feels as he joins the dawn attack
    - what he sees and hears in no man's land
    - how the attack progresses – any casualties or survivors

📖 Wider Reading

11. Read 'War Game', an award-winning short story by Michael Foreman. Compare the enthusiasm and excitement of the character Will with that of Eddie and John in the passage on the previous page, and then think about how these feelings change as the story progresses. What can we learn about war from these stories?

12. Visit the following sites for many personal stories and accounts of war:
    www.bbc.co.uk/ww2peopleswar
    and
    http://news.bbc.co.uk/1/hi/special_report/1998/10/98/world_war_i/197437.stm

Discussion

There is a fashion today for novels that tell stories about real life – family relationships, troubles at work, finding love, coping with illness, dealing with prejudice, and so on. Such topics may sound to you rather dismal subjects for a good story, but here you will find inspirational tales of courage and resilience as characters face – and overcome – their hardships.

The term 'social realism' is often used in this genre, and it means drama that reflects the realities of life – without being romanticised or softened. The way we all interact in society, as we all try to do the best we can with what we have been given, is a fascinating story in itself – and a rich source of ideas for authors.

In many ways, human interest stories reflect the life and times around us. When life-changing events occur around the world – like floods, earthquakes, famines or wars – storywriters will often seek to show, through their fictional stories, how these events affect the daily lives of ordinary people caught up in them.

We can learn a lot from human interest stories.

Focus

SETTING AND CONTEXT

- Human interest stories are about **real life**, so the settings are usually ordinary places that we might encounter everyday: home, school, work, towns and cities. Remember it is not their settings that makes these stories compelling; it is the lives of the people within them that are most interesting.
- The contexts for human interest stories often involve **everyday issues** and circumstances that many of us face in our own lives, for example: growing up, moving house, starting a new school, coping with bullies, overcoming illness, losing a family relative, and so on.
- The **social context** for a human interest story may range from a housing estate in a deprived neighbourhood, where life is tough and the opportunities to succeed are few, to a more privileged family, coping with a different sort of challenge.

○ ○ ● EXERCISE 1

Have there been any events in your own life – good or bad – that would make a good human interest story?

Share your thoughts and ideas with a friend. You don't have to delve into experiences that you would prefer to keep to yourself! Think of other moments when something interesting happened to you, which would be of interest to others.

○ ○ ● EXERCISE 2

Can you describe the places that form the 'backdrop' to your own life?

Working with a friend, take turns to write down a short description of the settings for your own life story. You may like to think about:

- the places where you have lived
- the schools you have attended
- where you have been on holiday
- where your friends and relatives live

You will probably notice that it is perhaps not the actual places themselves that are special – it is what happens in them!

CHARACTERS AND PLOT

- As you might expect, the **characters** in human interest stories are usually **ordinary people**, living ordinary lives. What makes them interesting is the way they cope with the issues and crises they face. As readers, we need to be able to identify with the characters we read about – to understand and sympathise with them – so there will be few superheroes or fantasy figures!

- The **relationships** between the characters are important here, and authors will describe the thoughts and feelings of the central characters each time they encounter new faces and new experiences. In human interest stories, we often become a 'friend and confidant' to the main characters.

- The **plot** in a human interest story may not be as complex or intricate as that of a crime novel, for example, where there needs to be an element of mystery or suspense, leading towards a climax at the end. Instead, events and situations will unfold in a way that reflects 'real time', like a 'day in the life' of someone you know, or an important period in childhood.

LANGUAGE AND STYLE

- The language used in stories of this kind is often informal – or **colloquial** which means ordinary or everyday, and this helps to create a life-like narrative. There will be some description – particularly to convey the thoughts and feelings of the main character or narrator – but you are unlikely to find great paragraphs of lyrical, figurative prose.

- Many human interest stories are written in the **first person narrative**, with the main character sharing his or her thoughts with the reader as they occur to them. This often makes for a light-hearted, conversational style of storytelling, like a friend recounting their experiences to you.

- The **present tense** is sometimes used in this genre, with a character's thoughts and responses revealed as a commentary, as the action unfolds around them.

●●● EXERCISE 3

Think of three people you know who would make interesting characters in a human interest story about your life. Then compile brief character descriptions, or 'profiles', for each one. You may like to think about:

- their appearance
- their personality
- how you know them/are related to them
- ways in which they have an impact or influence on your life

Once you have finished writing your notes, share them with the class.

●●● EXERCISE 4

A lot of human interest stories are about the dreams and aspirations that we all have, and how we can achieve them if we try.

Have you ever set yourself a goal and then worked very hard to achieve it? What else do you hope to achieve in the future? Think about music, sport, school work, hobbies, and perhaps future career plans.

The story of how you manage to reach your goals in life would make interesting reading. Share your past and future goals with a friend.

Sample

In his debut novel You Don't Know Me, *David Klass offers us a fascinating glimpse into the anxious and often frustrating world of adolescence. Does this sound like a typical teenager to you?*

You don't know me.

Just for example, you think I'm upstairs in my room doing my homework. Wrong. I'm not in my room. I'm not doing my homework. And even if I were up in my room I wouldn't be doing my homework, so you'd still be wrong. And it's really not my room. It's your room because it's in your house. I just happen to live there right now. And it's really not my homework, because my math teacher, Mrs Moonface, assigned it and she's going to check it, so it's her homework.

Her name's not Mrs Moonface, by the way. It's really Mrs Garlic Breath. No it's not. It's really Mrs Gabriel, but I just call her Mrs Garlic Breath, except for the times when I call her Mrs Moonface.

Confused? Deal with it.

You don't know me at all. You don't know the first thing about me. You don't know where I'm writing this from. You don't know what I look like. You have no power over me.

What do you think I like look like? Skinny? Freckles? Wire-rimmed glasses over brown eyes? No, I don't think so. Better look again. Deeper. It's like a kaleidoscope, isn't it? One minute I'm short, the next minute tall, one minute I'm geeky, one minute studly, my shape constantly changes, and the only thing that stays constant is my brown eyes. Watching you.

That's right, I'm watching you right now sitting on the couch next to the man who is not my father, pretending to read a book that is not a book, waiting for him to pet you like a dog or stroke you like a cat. Let's be real, the man who is not my father isn't a very nice man. Not just because he is not my father but because he hits me when you're not around, and he says if I tell you about it he'll really take care of me...

You don't know me at all.

You think I'm a good student. Hah!

You think I have friends. Hah!

You think I'm happy with this life. Hah, hah!

From *You Don't Know Me* by David Klass (Viking, 2001)

● ● ● EXERCISE 5

Discuss the following questions with a partner, or in a small group:

- In what ways is this excerpt more like a conversation than a story?
- How do you react to this kind of writing? What do you like/dislike about it?
- In the passage, the speaker asks the question, 'What do you think I look like?' In your group, discuss the images you each have in your mind. Are there any similarities in how you view the speaker?

❓ Questions

1a) Who do you think is speaking in the story?

  b) Who do you think this person is addressing?

2 How is it that the maths homework mentioned does not belong to the speaker?

3 What does this brief passage tell you about the speaker's relationship with his mother?

4 Do you think the speaker in the passage is jealous of the 'man who is not [his] father' because of the attention he receives from his mother? How can you tell?

5 Comment on the author's use of repetition throughout the passage. What effect does it have on the reader? Support your answer with evidence from the text.

6 This excerpt is taken from the beginning of the novel by David Klass. Why do you think the author has chosen to begin his story in this way? What kind of impression does it give of the lead character?

7 The lead character is an anxious adolescent, aggressive and yet insecure. How does the author convey this kind of personality? You will need to refer to:
   ● the choice of words used
   ● the conversational style of language
   ● the speaker's thoughts and feelings, shared with the reader

8 The narrator repeats the phrase 'you don't know me' throughout the passage. But do you think he actually knows himself? Try to explain your answer as fully as you can, with reference to the passage.

↔ Extension

9 How different would this story be if it had been written from the mother's point of view instead? Consider the mother's response to her son's plea, and write a similar piece of prose, this time from the mother's viewpoint, as she gazes out at her son, watching her from the garden. Does she know him well after all?

10 Write a similar passage of your own, in the style of the sample excerpt. This time choose a different person as the lead character, and place him or her in a different setting – perhaps at school or on a family holiday. Begin with 'You don't know me…'.

📖 Wider Reading

11 See if you can obtain a copy of *You Don't Know Me* by David Klass. You will find it an enjoyable read. As you progress through the story, think about how the author brings his main character to life and consider whether his view of teenage life is an accurate one!

12 Read other human interest stories that give you glimpses into the extraordinary lives of ordinary people. Some really good examples are:
The Curious Incident of the Dog in the Night-time by Mark Haddon (Red Fox, 2004)
Millions by Frank Cottrell Boyce (Harper Trophy, 2005)
Skellig by David Almond (Hodder Children's Books, 1998)
The Secret Diary of Adrian Mole Aged 13¾ by Sue Townsend (Penguin, 2002)

3.6 ADVENTURE

Discussion

Adventure stories thrill us. From tales of piracy and treason on the high seas, to epic journeys across mountains, jungles and deserts, this genre is full of excitement and escapism.

Some adventures may be real – there are plenty of true stories that can be thrilling when recounted by those involved – but many are fictional: packed with exciting characters, death-defying dangers, intriguing mysteries and, usually, glorious triumphs.

A good adventure story should whisk us away from our sofa or bed, (or school-desk), and take us to distant lands through vivid, page-turning prose.

●●● EXERCISE 1

Discuss with a partner any adventure stories you have found particularly thrilling.

Think about why you enjoyed each story. You may like to consider:

• the interesting settings
• the colourful characters
• the thrilling plot
• any exciting challenges faced
• the glorious ending

Focus

SETTING AND CONTEXT

• There are as many **different settings** for adventure stories as there are different landscapes on the Earth (and beyond it!). You may have read about sea voyages, mountain climbs, desert expeditions, jungle treks and so on. The important thing is to have a setting that offers a rich source of **challenges**, **dangers** and **thrills**.

• The word 'setting' can also mean the **time** in which a story is set, e.g. a seventeenth century sea voyage, or a 1930s mountain expedition. Each period of history may provide an interesting backdrop to the adventure, with different technologies, traditions and customs.

• The context for an adventure story may be some great **challenge** or **crisis** that must be faced, e.g. a voyage to find a treasure island (see excerpt overleaf) or a rescue mission. There may be wider circumstances too, that can affect the adventure, like a civil war or a natural disaster, for example.

●●● EXERCISE 2

If you could go on an adventure with your friends, where would you most like to go? What kind of challenges would you like to face?

Share your thoughts with a friend.

CHARACTERS AND PLOT

- Adventure stories traditionally offer a rich variety of interesting characters that gradually emerge along the hero's journey or quest. Some characters will be **helpful** – like a wise old sage or an expert of some kind – while others may **obstructive** or even threaten the hero of the story. When studying adventure stories, pay special attention to the way an author brings characters to life through **description**, **dialogue** and the **reactions** of others.

- Essential to every good adventure story is a thrilling plot that has a clear **direction** and **purpose** – a mountain rescue, a voyage of discovery or a trip up the Amazon, for example. Along the way, there may be **sub-plots** and events that threaten to take the hero away from the original goal. Some adventure stories may have several plots running in parallel, each one focusing on a different character's progress towards the same goal – just like Tolkien's *Lord of the Rings*.

● ● ● **EXERCISE 3**

Divide into groups of about three or four. Think of some adventure stories you have enjoyed. Then consider the plot in each one. Ask yourselves the following questions:

- Was there a stated goal or purpose to the plot?
- Did the hero(es) achieve this goal?
- Was there trouble along the way?
- Were some characters helpful, while others were not?

Share your ideas, dealing with each question in turn and listening to each other's views.

LANGUAGE AND STYLE

- When reading and studying adventure stories, you will notice that many are written using the **first person narrative** (*I set off on my quest...*) and may take the form of a **diary** or **recount** – just like an expedition record or a captain's log.

- Adventure stories are usually full of thrilling **action** and **suspense**. Though traditional adventures may still have long passages of rich description, many modern adventure stories focus more on fast-paced action, favouring short sections of **dialogue** and **narration** rather than detailed descriptions and characterisation.

- Some adventure stories – like the one featured on the following page – use well-known storytelling words and phrases to set the scene and move the narration along, like, *it all began...*, *by nightfall we had reached...* and *the next morning...*

- Most importantly, adventure stories provide a thrilling – and addictive – read, and authors work hard to hold readers' interest by creating dramatic effect through short and long sentences, punchy dialogue, powerful adjectives, and lots of fresh similes and metaphors.

Sample

One of the most famous adventure stories of them all is Treasure Island, *by Robert Louis Stevenson. In this short extract, young Jim Hawkins is running from the evil clutches of the notorious Long John Silver when he encounters an even stranger figure: the ragged Ben Gunn...*

From the side of the hill, which was here steep and stony, a spout of gravel was dislodged, and fell rattling and bounding through the trees. My eyes turned instinctively in that direction, and I saw a figure leap with great rapidity behind the trunk of a pine. What it was, whether bear or man or monkey, I could in no wise tell. It seemed dark and shaggy; more I knew not. But the terror of this new apparition brought me to a stand.

I was now, it seemed, cut off upon both sides; behind me the murderers, before me this lurking nondescript. And immediately I began to prefer the dangers that I knew to those I knew not. Silver himself appeared less terrible in contrast with this creature of the woods, and I turned on my heel, and, looking sharply behind me over my shoulder, began to retrace my steps in the direction of the boats.

Instantly the figure reappeared, and, making a wide circuit, began to head me off. I was tired, at any rate; but had I been as fresh as when I rose, I could see it was in vain for me to contend in speed with such an adversary. From trunk to trunk the creature flitted like a deer, running manlike on two legs, but unlike any man that I had ever seen, stooping almost double as it ran. Yet a man it was, I could no longer be in doubt about that.

I began to recall what I had heard of cannibals. I was within an ace of calling for help. But the mere fact that he was a man, however wild, had somewhat reassured me, and my fear of Silver began to revive in proportion. I stood still, therefore, and cast about for some method of escape; and as I was so thinking, the recollection of my pistol flashed into my mind. As soon as I remembered I was not defenceless, courage glowed again in my heart; and I set my face resolutely for this man of the island, and walked briskly towards him.

He was concealed by this time, behind another tree trunk; but he must have been watching me closely, for as soon as I began to move in his direction he reappeared and took a step to meet me. Then he hesitated, drew back, came forward again, and at last, to my wonder and confusion, threw himself on his knees and held out his clasped hands in supplication.

At that I once more stopped.

'Who are you?' I asked.

'Ben Gunn,' he answered, and his voice sounded hoarse and awkward, like a rusty lock. 'I'm poor Ben Gunn, I am; and I haven't spoke with a Christian these three years.'

I could now see that he was a white man like myself, and that his features were even pleasing. His skin, wherever it was exposed, was burnt by the sun; even his lips were black; and his fair eyes looked quite startling in so dark a face. Of all the beggar-men that I had seen or fancied, he was the chief for raggedness. He was clothed with tatters of old ship's canvas and old sea cloth; and this extraordinary patchwork was all held together by a system of the most various and incongruous fastenings, brass buttons, bits of stick, and loops of tarry gaskin. About his waist he wore an old brass-buckled leather belt, which was the one thing solid in his whole accoutrement.

'Three years!' I cried. 'Were you shipwrecked?'

'Nay, mate,' said he – 'marooned.'

From *Treasure Island* by Robert Louis Stevenson (Puffin, 1994)

● ● ● EXERCISE 4

The above passage is written in the first person narrative, from the narrator's viewpoint. How different might it have seemed if it had been written in the third person? Do you think something may have been lost in terms of excitement and suspense?

With a partner, take turns in narrating a paragraph each, changing the first person to the third person narrative as you read it aloud (i.e. *I saw a figure* will become *he saw a figure*).

What has changed?

Questions

1 What was it that first caught Jim's attention and revealed the figure to him?

2 There is a well-known phrase which goes, 'better the devil you know than the devil you don't'. How is this particularly appropriate here?

3 Find a word or phrase that highlights the stranger's animal-like agility.

4 What was it that enabled Jim to regain his courage?

5 Rephrase the following in your own words, retaining the same meaning as far as possible: 'my fear of Silver began to revive in proportion'.

6 The stranger eventually surrenders himself to Jim, falling on his knees before him. Describe, in your own words, Jim's reaction to this. What was he expecting?

7 *Treasure Island*, from which this excerpt was taken, was published in 1883. Find two brief examples of traditional language used in the passage which might suggest to you that it was written more than a century ago.

 # Extension

8 Comment on the ways in which the author develops our interest in the character, Ben Gunn.

9 Write a similar passage of your own, in which you narrate the story from Ben Gunn's point of view, as he first sees the young stranger – after being marooned on the island for years. You may like to consider:
- whether Gunn feels threatened by Hawkins
- the appearance of Jim – you may use your imagination here
- Gunn's relief at finding that the young stranger means no harm

10 Imagine that Jim Hawkins returns to the ship from which he came. Write a conversation he might have with his captain, in which he describes the stranger he met on the island.

 # Wider Reading

11 Obtain a copy of Robert Louis Stevenson's classic adventure story, *Treasure Island*, and find out what happens to Jim Hawkins. There are also several play versions of the story, including one dramatised by David Calcutt (Oxford University Press, 2002). The story was made into several films too.

12 You can access lots of interesting information about Stevenson's original novel from the following website:
www.ukoln.ac.uk/services/treasure
A general synopsis and full set of chapter summaries for *Treasure Island* can be viewed at the following sites:
www.online-literature.com/stevenson/
    treasureisland
www.bibliomania.com/0/0/46/88/
    frameset.html

PROSE

Writing

UNIT 4
WRITING ESSAYS

INTRODUCTION

Examination requirements

In this unit you will develop the skills needed to tackle the first section of the writing paper for Common Entrance, currently entitled 'Studied Literature'.

Under Studied Literature you will find four essay questions, from which you must choose one. Two questions will be based on the set theme for your literature studies. These questions will require you to explore a particular aspect of the theme, illustrating your comments with specific reference to one or more set texts you have studied in class. These class texts will have been carefully chosen by your teacher for their close links to the current literature studies theme.

There will be two other questions which are not based on the set theme for your studies, but are concerned with more general literary themes, techniques or preferences. You will still need to refer to one or more texts you have studied when answering these questions.

Whichever question you choose to answer, you will need to put down your response in the form of an **essay**.

What is an essay?

An essay is, quite simply, a piece of writing on a particular subject. In a literary essay – like the one you will need to write in the exam – the 'subject' will be a theme taken from the stories, plays or poems that you have studied.

An essay can serve several different purposes; it may:

- compare and contrast opposing views about something
- offer personal opinions and comments
- consider how a particular theme is developed through a story
- focus on a specific event and consider its impact
- discuss the role that a particular character plays in a story

Whatever the focus, an essay is an opportunity for you to 'say what you think', and provided you are able to support your views with evidence from the text, then you cannot go far wrong.

However... essay questions are often greeted with some trepidation by many of us, precisely because they do not ask for straightforward answers, preferring to use words and phrases like 'discuss...', 'respond to...' or 'comment on...'. These words offer no clues as to where to find the answers. They are personal; they are about *you* and what you *think*.

To write a good essay you need to be: **organised**, **articulate** and **thorough**. You need to remain focused on the question at all times and remember that every point you choose to make needs to be accompanied by evidence that supports it – in the form of quotations or broad references to events and characters from books.

Most essays follow the same format, and are made up of the same kind of features, which are listed below.

Remember: one of the most important ingredients needed to make a successful essay is something you should have an endless supply of... **opinions**.

● ● ● ● **EXERCISE 1**

How do we actually form an opinion? Are we influenced by the views of friends around us? How many of us grow up to believe what our parents believe?

Working in small groups, share your opinions in response to each of these statements. Spend just a few moments on each one, allowing everyone to say what they think.

1 'The character of Harry Potter sets a bad example for today's children.'

2 'Making books into films, like the *Lord of the Rings* trilogy, spoils the imaginations of all of us.'

3 'Phillip Pullman's *Northern Lights* is the best children's book of modern times.'

Did you agree or disagree with the statements in Exercise 1? Did you share your opinions? Did anyone ask you to explain your views? Is it enough just to say you don't like something without explaining why? Think about it...

Once you have decided what you think, you need to consider how best to put your views down on paper in a clear and logical way. You need to think about how your essay should be structured.

FEATURES OF AN ESSAY

Most essays are made up of the following features:

● an introduction
● a discussion
● a conclusion

The introduction

It is important to begin an essay by demonstrating that you understand the question you are being asked, and the terms that are used within it. So this means you need to start with some definitions. Take the following example, from a past Common Entrance Paper:

Choose one or more of your studied texts and, by referring carefully to events which take place, discuss to what extent the central character deserves to be called a hero or heroine.

© Independent Schools Examinations Board

To answer this question properly, you need to begin by demonstrating what is meant by the term *hero* or *heroine*. Once you have shown that you know what a hero is, you can then judge whether a fictional character deserves to be called one.

Once you have defined the key terms used in the question, and then stated which book – and which particular character – you are discussing, you need to **answer the question**. It may seem premature to do this, especially as you have barely started the essay (and you don't want to run out of things to say), but it is a good idea to set out your opinion at the beginning. You can then move on to illustrating and supporting this opinion with actual examples from the text.

So, taking the sample question above, you might state straightaway that the character you have chosen certainly deserves the name 'hero'. In the next section, you can then discuss why you believe this to be the case.

● ● ● EXERCISE 2

A hero (or heroine if it is a female) is someone who is admired for their courage and for what they have achieved. But what else makes a hero? In pairs, discuss the qualities we look for in our heroes and heroines?

Share your thoughts with the class, and then compile a character profile for a hero, listing the most important qualities, strengths and skills, needed for the job.

Remember, you should be able to explain why you have listed each quality. You must be able to share your opinion about it!

The discussion

This is the main part of any essay – the 'meat' sandwiched between the introduction and the conclusion.

The question is, how can a 'discussion' – which we might usually think of as a spoken conversation between two or more people – take place on paper, with only one person expressing a view?

Many essay questions contain the word 'discuss'. What this actually means is: share your views about something and then share *how* and *why* you came to hold these views. The 'discussion' takes place between you and the reader, even though the reader can only listen!

Once you have stated your view with a sentence or two that directly tackles the question, you then need to give **examples** from the text that support what you say, discussing each one and showing how it proves your point. So, continuing with the sample question, you would then need to cite some examples from your chosen text in which your character can be seen displaying some heroic qualities – and therefore deserves to be called a hero, thus proving your point.

Remember: your views are important, whatever you may think, and the only opinion that can be 'wrong' is the one that carries no **evidence** to support it.

The conclusion

Every good essay, no matter how brief, needs a conclusion, in which the **views** you have given, the **points** you have made, and the **evidence** you have included are drawn together. You can then revisit the question and answer it again.

Writing a conclusion ensures that you return to the question. There is nothing worse than writing – or reading – an essay that meanders aimlessly away from the central question and ends in a different place from where it started. Keep sharp, stay relevant and try to show that you have understood both the question and your answer to it.

● ● ● EXERCISE 3

Can you think of a book character who deserves to be called a hero or heroine?

In pairs or small groups, take turns in explaining why your chosen character should be regarded as a hero. Remember to give reasons, backed up with examples from the book.

USING EVIDENCE

In some examinations students are allowed to bring set texts into the room, and then use them to supply quotations when tackling essay questions. In the Common Entrance English Examinations, however, this is not permitted. So your approach to the inclusion of evidence is going to be different – because it would be impossible to memorise a whole reading book and select quotes from memory!

If, having chosen your essay question, a short quotation from a studied text comes to mind, then use it in your essay, to illustrate a point you are making. (Remember to put quotation marks around the actual words). However, what is more likely is that you will refer broadly to events and characters from a story, using your own words.

In the case of the sample question on page 100, you would need to give actual examples from your chosen book that demonstrate your character's heroism – you need to 'catch him or her being heroic'. When you recall actual events, situations and circumstances in the plot, you are achieving three things:

- you are proving you have read and understood the book
- you are showing you are able to select appropriate and relevant evidence from a text
- you are supporting the points you make, i.e. proving you are right!

Phrases like, 'at the beginning of the story', 'later on in the book', and 'as the plot develops' are useful when incorporating evidence of this kind into your essays.

Remember: most of the time quotation marks will not be necessary because you are only referring to, and discussing, the events and characters in the story, you are not actually quoting from it.

When selecting evidence from a book to help you tackle a literary essay question, you may like to consider:

- important events in the plot
- characterisation (description and development of characters)
- use of imagery
- interesting dialogue
- setting

RANGE OF THEMES

Two of the questions available in the Studied Literature section of the Common Entrance (CE) writing paper are based on a set theme. You may already have studied one or two set texts in class which are based on the current theme, and no doubt you will study several more. This theme is set for a few years, after which it changes again to a new theme.

In this unit you will encounter many sample essay questions. These are arranged into sample themes, some of which have been real CE themes in the past, others may be used in the future.

These themes include:

- Relationships (i): Love
- Relationships (ii): Friendship
- Heroes and heroines
- Conflict
- Freedom
- Ambition

These are very broad themes, and they allow for a wide range of books to be studied in your classes. Whether you are focusing on conflict or love, freedom or ambition, the process of studying and writing essays on a literary theme will be the same.

How good is your book knowledge? How well-read are you?

Working in pairs, see if you can come up with three recommended books for each of the themes on the previous page. Choose books that explore the themes within their stories.

HOW TO FOCUS ON A THEME

As you progress through this unit, you will need to think about how each literary theme is explored in the novels and short stories you read.

But how do you focus on a theme as vast as 'love' or 'conflict'? How do you then 'talk about' the theme in an essay? Where do you begin?

The answer is that you consider the different ways in which the themes make themselves visible in stories. You need to look at:

- the characters involved
- any actions and events
- the language used
- any morals or messages offered

Taking 'love' as an example of a broad theme, look out for:

- characters that give love, or feel unloved
- actions and events that are influenced by the presence, or absence, of love
- descriptive language that describes love
- any lessons that can be learned about love

This is how themes are explored in books. And this is where you will find the evidence you need to fill your essays. To help you along the way, each section in this unit uses the same approach to focus on a different literary theme. Each time, you will look at characters encountered, actions and events that take place, language used and morals or messages offered.

Final word...

Writing essays is not an easy process. There will be times when you wish for a question that requires a shorter, more straightforward answer. But as you get better at it, you will find that essays aren't so bad. They are ideal opportunities for you to say what you think. Just remember the golden rules:

● ● ● EXERCISE 5

Think about a book you have read recently in which the theme of 'love' plays an important part in the story. With a partner, discuss where, and how, this theme appears. What effect does love have on the characters, actions and events in the story?

How does this theme come through in the language used?

Are there any lessons you can learn about love from what happens in the story?

- Read the question carefully
- Choose a book that you know a lot about and is appropriate for the theme
- Answer the question
- Support your comments with good evidence
- Stay on course, don't meander!

Discussion

Is there any other literary theme that is greater, or more widely explored in novels than love? It is love, of course, that gives rise to so many different tensions, emotions and experiences, from jealousy and pain to happiness and companionship, from the thrill of one's first relationship, to the pain of losing a loved one. No wonder, then, that authors incorporate love into their stories.

Love stories can comfort us, amuse us, anger and frustrate us, or even teach us some valuable lessons. Successful authors can recreate situations in their novels with which readers may be able to identify, because they remind them of experiences they may have had in their own lives – good or bad!

Just like friendship, love is a literary theme that gives life to fictional characters, giving them emotions and passions that we can all identify with at some stage in our lives. Just as in real life, the characters in stories may do anything in the name of love.

In the stories you discussed together in Exercise 1, how were the characters' feelings put across by the authors? Even though you may not have shared the same feelings as the fictional characters, were you able to understand and sympathise with them? Were their feelings genuine?

The way in which feelings of love, anger, jealousy and hate are brought out in characters is something that is worth studying. For it is when we see fictional characters reacting to difficult situations and responding with 'real' feeling to what is happening around them that we then start to believe they are real – and we enjoy the story so much more.

Think how we, as real people, show our feelings – through our actions, what we say, what we don't say, and what we think. And so it is with fictional characters.

●●● EXERCISE 1

Can you think of some stories you have read in which love affects the way the characters feel and act? Does love make them jealous, overjoyed, concerned or angry? What does love drive them to do?

Share your reading experiences with a partner.

Focus

CHARACTERS

- Love as a literary theme is vast, and the range of characters who give and receive love in stories may be infinite. What they may share in common is that the love they feel may drive them on – a love for a partner, a family member, a beloved pet, a religion, or even a country.
- Consider how each author describes the feelings of the fictional characters. How do they attribute real emotions to them in ways that are convincing? How do you know when the love someone feels is real?

ACTIONS AND EVENTS

- When studying novels that explore the literary theme of love, think about how the actions of the characters involved are influenced by the love they feel. Does love cause rifts between people? Or is love the unifying force that binds them together?
- Think too about the events that unfold in the novel. Are they the result of love, or the absence of it? Are there different events in the story that test the love felt by characters, in the same way that friendship or heroism may be tested?

● ● ● EXERCISE 2

There have been so many stories, plays, poems and songs written on the theme of love that it seems difficult to imagine new words and phrases to describe characters who are in love. But it is possible...

With a partner, think up some new similes and metaphors to describe the love someone might feel for a partner, family member or beloved pet. Here are some to start you off:

- *Their love bound them together, like a warm blanket on a snowy day...*
- *Love set her free, like a butterfly rising from its cocoon...*
- *When he was away from her, his heart became a hollow shell, through which the cold wind rattled...*

● ● ● EXERCISE 3

Think of some stories in which love plays a central part. How does it shape the plot? Are there some events in the story that happen only because of the love that someone feels – or ceases to feel – for another?

Think about it and share your opinions with a friend.

LANGUAGE

- The language that authors use to convey the love felt by their characters varies greatly, and can range from traditional, romantic prose, full of rich similes and metaphors (e.g. *My love for thee is a burning fire...*), to more simple, contemporary phrasing that is less figurative but equally moving (*You make me whole...*).
- Similarly, the way in which authors construct and vary the length of their sentences can create dramatic effect where love is felt by a character (e.g. *Softly, like a petal on the breeze, she floated across the room towards me. I froze.*).

MORALS AND MESSAGES

- Loving relationships need to be worked at; it is not all plain-sailing. When reading stories on this theme, think about the messages authors are conveying about love, commitment, loyalty, sacrifices and so on.
- Consider too how the authors convey moral lessons. If love breaks down in a story, are there some characters who are at fault, and others who have been wronged? Who is to blame? Can love overcome all conflicts?

●●● EXERCISE 4

Working with a partner, look at the following phrases and sentences and decide whether they belong in traditional romantic prose or a more modern novel. Try to identify what it is that makes each one seem modern or old.

- My love for thee is everlasting
- You're everything to me
- My heart is all aflutter
- I'm falling for you
- My world revolves around you
- Parting is such sweet sorrow
- Marry me!
- I confess my undying love for thee

Do you think saying it in modern language loses impact? Or does traditional prose seem clichéd now? How, and why, has the fashion changed?

●●● EXERCISE 5

With a partner, think of some stories you have read in which the love that characters feel for one another has been truly tested. This may be through conflict, suffering, misunderstanding or misfortune.

Did the love survive? Did it actually become stronger as a result?

ESSAYS

Model Essay

QUESTION

A person who has lost a loved one may find it very hard to love again. By referring to one or more stories you have read, show how an author teaches us that loneliness and sorrow can fade in time and make way for happiness and companionship once more.

Read the following essay, which may be regarded as one way to tackle this question. There are other ways. Remember, in a Common Entrance Examination, you will not be permitted to take your set texts in with you. This means that you are not expected to quote directly from books, although if quotations occur to you, you may include them. Instead, you will be required to make reference to the events and characters they feature. You will not have much time, so your essay will need to be concise.

Introduction to reiterate the central point of the question – and to show that you understand.	There are many stories that deal with the tragedy of losing a loved one. The effects of such a loss can be devastating on those who are left to grieve. But love can be found again, sometimes when you least expect it.

Introduce the character(s) you will be focusing on.

An example of a character who suffers a tragic loss and then eventually finds someone else to love can be found in Michelle Magorian's classic story, 'Goodnight Mister Tom'.

Set the scene by explaining how, and why, Tom has become lonely and grief-stricken.

In this story, we meet Tom Oakley, a lonely and embittered old man, living in a small village in the countryside during the second world war. Tom is known throughout the village for his abrasive manner and lack of interest in other people. But there is a reason why he feels this way: whilst fighting on board ship during the first world war, Tom's young wife and baby son, back in England, caught Scarlet Fever and tragically died. They had already been buried by the time he returned home.

That was many years ago and now, as an old man, Tom's grief has steadily eaten away at his soul, leaving an empty shell of a person, reluctant to let anyone else close to him, perhaps for fear that he may lose them also.

Further explanation of Tom's grief – setting the scene for what follows.

Introduce second character.

But one morning, there is a knock at his door and moments later he faces the prospect of looking after a young evacuee from the city, billeted out to the countryside for safety, away from the bombing raids over London.

Young William Beech is about ten years old. He has had to endure a terrible childhood of poverty and neglect in the back streets of London. His mother is cruel to him. He does not know who, or where, his father is. Like Tom, William is shy and very nervous around strangers – for equally obvious reasons.

As the story progresses, so Tom and William gradually find some common ground. There are many similarities between the two characters: William has lived without proper love in his life for as long as he can remember; and Tom has been a widower for many years too. When William hears the news that his mother has died, he too is alone in the world.

Against the expectations of all who know Tom, and perhaps surprising even himself, he grows to love the child as if he were his own flesh and blood.

No one thought that Tom could learn to welcome someone into his heart again, least of all Tom himself. Perhaps the most moving point comes when William first calls Tom 'Dad'. Tom didn't notice at first. It was only later when he was in bed that the significance of William's words dawned on him. Tears of happiness ran down his cheeks.

By the end of the story, Tom has been allowed to adopt William as his own son, thus confirming that he is now ready to let someone into his heart for good. His loneliness and sorrow have faded and made way for happiness and companionship once again.

> Show how friendship grows between the characters – breaking down barriers.

> Conclude with demonstration of Tom's ability to love again.

> Return to the words of the question in the final sentence.

●●● EXERCISE 6

Based on your knowledge of this well-known book (which was also made into a hugely successful film), do you think Tom needed William as much as the young boy needed Tom?

Explain your ideas as clearly as you can in conversation with a friend.

❓ Essay Questions (Relationships: love)

1 'Love can heal wounds, but it can also cause pain.' Discuss this statement, with reference to at least one text you have read, in which the power of love is demonstrated.

2 'People will often do the most remarkable things in the name of love.' Have you found this to be true in one or more of the books you have read? Discuss at least one example of a fictional character doing something extraordinary because of the love they feel for another.

3 They say that absence makes the heart grow fonder. Using one or more texts you have read, show how authors demonstrate this through the situations in which they place their characters.

4 With reference to one or more texts you have studied, show how an author might convey the strong bond between a mother and her child.

5 Write an essay recommending a good story you have read in which two characters fall in love, against the wishes of their family and friends.

6 Referring to at least one story you have read, show how an author demonstrates the old maxim 'love is blind'.

7 Just like friendship, love can sometimes be put to the test – and fail. Refer to at least one book you have studied in which a love is left wanting when it really mattered.

↔ Extended Writing Questions

8 Are you patriotic? Do you love your country? Are you proud of where you come from? Write an essay in which you describe the things you love – and the things you dislike – about the country you are from.

9 What is love? Such a question has often been asked! Write a short essay in which you explain what the term 'love' means for you.

10 Write an original story in which a character has to sacrifice something important to them for the sake of love. This may be giving up a favourite hobby; moving from a favourite place to a new house in order to be with someone; or changing jobs, for example.

Wider Reading

11 Read Anne Fine's *Flour Babies*. Then write an essay in which you describe some of the lessons which the main character, Simon Martin, learns about a parent's love, from the strange school project which he must complete.

12 The following texts explore the theme of Love:
- *Romeo and Juliet* by William Shakespeare (Penguin, 1994)
- *Flour Babies* by Anne Fine (Puffin, 1994)
- *Coram Boy* by Jamila Gavin (Egmont, 2004)
- *Northern Lights* by Phillip Pullman (Scholastic, 2005)
- *Goodnight Mister Tom* by Michelle Magorian (Puffin, 1983)
- *Oliver Twist* by Charles Dickens (Penguin, 1994)
- *Cider with Rosie* by Laurie Lee (Vintage, 2002)
- *You Don't Know Me* by David Klass (Viking, 2001)
- *Birdsong* by Sebastian Faulks (Vintage, 1994)
- *Angela's Ashes* by Frank McCourt (HarperPerennial, 2005)

Discussion

Building and keeping friendships is an important part of life for most people. Many of us need friends to share the good times and to provide comfort and support when life is tough. The subject of friendship can be a rich source of drama and interest for many authors to explore in the stories they write. Joy, sadness, jealousy and pride are just some of the recurring features of friendship.

When reading about fictional friendships, think about how authors build realistic relationships between their characters. What do the friends have in common? Do they have different personalities? In what ways do they complement one another? What is it that makes them seem like friends?

It is often said that when people fall on hard times, they know who their true friends are – meaning some friends are only around when times are good. When the chips are down and a person needs help, superficial friends may not be found.

The same is true for fictional characters in stories. Authors will often put friendships to the test – dreaming up situations that may divide loyalties, cause jealousy or create competition between friends. This is where the drama lies.

Focus

CHARACTERS

- Friendships are often formed when two or more people share the same interests, hobbies or opinions. We call them 'kindred spirits' or like-minded people. In stories, look at the similarities and differences between the characters. Is a friendship destined to last or does it look like there may be friction or even conflict due to differences of opinion?

- Unlike in real life, in fictional worlds, friendships are never private – that is to say the reader is involved too. He or she is privy to what each friend thinks of the other. When reading about friendships in stories, consider how the authors convey the thoughts and feelings of friends. Do they really like one another?

●●● EXERCISE 1

What does the word *friend* mean to you?

Working in small groups, come up with a brief definition for the term friend. Can you explain it in a sentence or two?

Share definitions with the class and then vote for the best one.

●●● EXERCISE 2

Return to your earlier definitions of what a friend means to you. Working in similar or different groups this time, make a list of all the characteristics you might expect to find in a good friend (*e.g. good listener, patient, good sense of humour, supportive*).

Then try to answer the following questions:

- Are you a good friend? How many of these characteristics do you think you have?
- How many do your friends have?
- If your best friend had to lose three of these friendly characteristics, which ones would you be happy for him or her to lose?

ACTIONS AND EVENTS

- When studying the theme of friendship in literary texts, look at how the characters' actions are influenced by the friends they keep. They may be trying to impress friends, mimic them, protect them, or perhaps even make them jealous. We are all often influenced by our friends, so consider how authors reflect this in their writing.
- Sometimes the events that unfold in stories are designed to test the bonds of friendship between certain characters. This is how stories can be exciting. Events may take place which cause divided loyalties, with difficult decisions to be faced to avoid others being hurt.

LANGUAGE

- When reading about fictional friendships, think about how authors recreate the friendliness through dialogue. How do the friends refer to one another? Are there certain phrases which they often use – from shared jokes, perhaps? How does the author create the informal and easy way in which friends usually converse – sometimes called 'banter'?
- As mentioned earlier in this chapter, fictional friendships are never private, because the reader is always present. Consider, then, how each character may feel about his or her friend(s); what sort of names do they give them? What adjectives are used to describe them?

MORALS AND MESSAGES

- Many stories of friendship can teach us the importance of standing by our friends. But how are these messages conveyed to us? Authors may create scenes in which friends fail to support one another and we see the upset is caused. We may also see the negative effects that jealousy or resentment can have on a fictional friendship.
- Authors may share with us how characters feel when they have been let down by their friends. Similarly, we may learn how much pleasure and comfort can be found when friendships are kept. Reading about fictional friends in stories might remind you to look after your own friends.

●●● EXERCISE 3

Have you ever faced a situation in which supporting one friend caused upset to another?

With a partner, or in small groups, discuss the idea of divided loyalties. What can one do in such cases? Should a real friend put you in a situation where you have to choose? Share your thoughts.

●●● EXERCISE 4

How many different ways of greeting someone can you think of? Does it depend on the situation and how well you know each person?

Meeting a business associate for the first time, you are unlikely to say 'alright mate?'. On the other hand, when greeting a friend in the park, it would seem strange to say 'good evening sir'.

With a partner, list all the informal and formal greetings you can think of. Which of these might be exchanged between fictional friends?

●●● EXERCISE 5

Has there been a time when you have been glad to have a friend? How did you feel?

Working in pairs, write two columns of words: the first is a list of 'positive' adjectives to describe how you feel when surrounded by friends; the second is a list of 'negative' adjectives to show how you may feel without any friends.

You could begin with:

Positive	Negative
comforted	alone
entertained	lost

Model Essay

QUESTION

'A true friend is someone you can confide in without fear of being judged or betrayed.' Write about one example of a friend confiding in another in a story you have read.

Read the following essay, which may be regarded as one way to tackle this question. There are other ways. Remember, in a Common Entrance Examination, you will not be permitted to take your set texts in with you. This means that you are not expected to quote directly from books, although if quotations occur to you, you may include them. Instead, you will be required to make reference to the events and characters they feature. You will not have much time, so your essay will need to be concise.

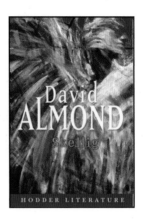

Introduction to show that you understand the question.

It is always good to have a friend in whom you can confide. A true friend is a good listener – one with whom you can share your thoughts and feelings without worrying whether they will judge you or tell other people about you. You should be able to trust a friend, particularly when you are in need of someone to share your problems with.

In 'Skellig', by David Almond, the main character, Michael, is in need of a good friend. He feels unsettled, having moved to a strange new house in a strange street. He also feels helpless and alone, as he watches his parents cope with the terrible strain of watching his baby sister fight for her life in a hospital bed.

Move on to introduce your chosen book and main character.

Show why the character needs a friend to confide in. Keep the commentary very brief!

Then he finds a stranger in his garage: an extraordinary character, whom he mistakes for a crippled old man. He considers telling his parents about the old man in the garage, but they are so preoccupied with his baby sister that there is never the right moment.

Then he meets Mina, a girl who lives on the same street. In many ways she is so different from Michael: confident, knowledgeable, creative and curious. She inspires him. She does not go to school – her mother teaches her at home instead. She does not seem to have – or need – many friends of her own. She is independent. But Michael likes her. He likes her worldly open-mindedness and her 'eyes that seem to see straight through you'.

Introduce and describe the friend in whom Michael confides.

ESSAYS

Describes how he confides in her – and why he trusts her.

Soon he confides in her. He shares his concerns about his baby sister. Then he shares his secret – he takes her to meet 'Skellig', the old man in the garage. He believes she is clever and will know what to do. No one else would have believed him. His friends at school already think he is quite odd, and telling them about the stranger in the garage would only have convinced them further. They even tease him for spending time with the 'monkey girl' as they call her. But as his friendship with Mina grows, he finds that he can trust her. She always says the right thing.

When Michael first tells Mina about the 'thing' in the garage, he is not even sure if he dreamt it up. He seems confused, but Mina comforts and assures him that 'truth and dreams are always getting muddled anyway'.

She helps him move Skellig to an old derelict and boarded up house in another street, arranging to meet up at dawn by using their own secret owl calling, which Michael teaches her.

Describe the benefits of having a friend to confide in – and what his life would be like without Mina.

Mina never betrays Michael's trust. She listens to him. Sometimes she advises him, or just amuses him with her extraordinary knowledge. In many ways, it is Mina who helps Michael to cope with what is a very stressful time for him, and his family. Without Mina, Michael would feel very isolated – and would certainly not know what to do with Skellig.

By the end of the story, we discover that Skellig is actually an angel, his twisted and bent limbs are actually wings. Mina has shared in this wondrous secret. Indeed in the final chapter, Michael is convinced that, in the evening light, he can see wings attached to Mina too.

In the conclusion show why he is right to trust in Mina – i.e. she is an angel too!

● ● ● EXERCISE 6

Are you familiar with David Almond's *Skellig*?

If you have read it, find someone in the class who has not and then explain to them what the story is about – and what you thought of it.

Did you ever imagine that the old man in the garage was going to be an angel? What clues were there in the story to suggest that he might have been?

? Essay Questions (Friendship)

1 Referring to one or more texts you have read, illustrate how authors like to test the friendships of their fictional characters by placing them in difficult situations.

2 'Only when you are in trouble can you know who your real friends are.' Discuss this statement, highlighting one or two examples from books you have read in which friends support or desert one another.

3 'Good friendships need time to develop.' Have you found this to be true in the stories you have read? Refer to one or more texts and show how fictional friendships have flourished over time.

4 Lasting friendships do not always come easily: they often require work and commitment from both parties. Referring to one or more texts you have read, show how an author illustrates the highs and the lows of keeping a friendship going.

5 Demonstrate, by referring to one or more fictional friendships, how important it is to stick by your friends in times of trouble.

6 They say opposites often attract. Can you think of one or more fictional friendships that prove this theory? By referring to one or more texts you have read, illustrate how people who appear to be very different may enjoy lasting friendships with one another.

7 'A dog is a man's best friend.' Pets often make super friends, particularly for those who lack the opportunity to go out and meet new people. Referring to one or more stories you have read, illustrate how an animal can be an ideal companion for a person.

↔ Extended Writing Questions

8 Think of a story you have read that features a close friendship between two characters.

Write a short piece, in role as one of the characters, in which you explain why your friend is so important to you.

9 Write an essay in which you describe the importance of friendship – and why we must never take our friends for granted.

10 Friendships at school and at home are important, but sometimes peers can exert pressure on us to say or do things just because they are popular. Describe a time when you felt pressure from friends to do something that you did not really want to do. Did you resist? Should true friends influence us in this way?

📖 Wider Reading

11 Read John Steinbeck's classic story of friendship, entitled *Of Mice and Men*. Write an essay discussing the sacrifices made by George, in order to support his friend, Lennie.

12 The following texts explore the theme of Friendship:

- *Skellig* by David Almond (Hodder Children's Books, 1998)
- *Goodnight Mister Tom* by Michelle Magorian (Puffin, 1983)
- *The Adventures of Sherlock Holmes* by Arthur Conan Doyle (Penguin, 1981)
- *Lord of the Flies* by William Golding (Faber and Faber, 1997)
- *Smith* by Leon Garfield (Oxford University Press, 1997)
- *Northern Lights* by Phillip Pullman (Scholastic, 1998)
- *The Dolphin Crossing* by Jill Paton Walsh (Puffin, 1970)
- *Of Mice and Men* by John Steinbeck (Longman, 2000)
- *The Lord of the Rings* by J.R.R. Tolkien (Del Rey Books, 1989)
- *Stormbreaker* by Anthony Horowitz (Walker Books, 2005)
- *The Hound of the Baskervilles* by Arthur Conan Doyle (Penguin, 1996)

ESSAYS

4.3 Heroes and Heroines

 Discussion

From the great myths of the Ancient Greeks and Romans, to modern-day tales of conflicts and challenges, heroes and heroines feature frequently in stories. They give us something to aspire to; they fill us with hope; they show us that good *can* conquer evil, and courage *can* overcome adversity.

Heroism is a recurring theme in many novels and short stories. The heroes and heroines from some stories have become so well known that they may seem real to us.

●●●● **EXERCISE 1**

Working in small groups, make a list of well-known fictional heroes and heroines from the stories and plays you have read. You could begin with Frodo Baggins from *Lord of the Rings* or Lyra from *Northern Lights*.

Then think about what it is that makes these characters so heroic. Make a list of the qualities and skills which they may have in common.

But what does it mean to be a hero or heroine? What *is* heroism? In the exercise above, why did you choose each particular character? What qualities do they have that make them special? What actions have they taken, or what successes have they achieved that suggest they are heroic?

Heroic characters face dangers and challenges for us, while we follow their efforts from the comfort of our own armchairs.

But we often like our heroes to be 'only human', that is to say with weaknesses as well as strengths. If we are to aspire to be like the people we read about, then these characters need not be perfect in every way, for none of us could ever be that!

Focus

CHARACTERS

- Many readers aspire to being like the heroes they read about, but no one can ever be perfect, so for heroes to have universal appeal – and to seem realistic – authors may give them weaknesses as well as strengths. Look out for ways in which authors make their heroes vulnerable, to remind you that they are 'only human'. You may like to think about:
  - bad habits they may have, like drinking or smoking
  - a short temper
  - a particular fear, like vertigo or arachnophobia!
  - a tendency to be stubborn
- Can a story have a hero without a villain? This is a question that often arises when studying this theme. To provide balance, not to mention suspense, authors will usually pitch their heroes against some form of enemy. This may take the form of an individual (i.e. a person, alien or monster), or it may actually be a dangerous situation or disaster, like a volcano eruption or an earthquake that threatens the hero and those around him/her.

> ●●● EXERCISE 2
>
> Can you think of some famous literary villains and their opposing heroes? With a partner, make a list of some well-known adversaries.
>
> Then think about how these characters differ and what they may actually have in common. You may be surprised to find how similar they actually are!

ACTIONS AND EVENTS

- Some questions on this theme may ask you to focus on heroic acts that take place in the stories you have read. After all, a hero is not a hero until he has proven himself – either in battle, or in some other form of trouble or difficulty (called 'adversity'). When studying heroes, look at the way they act in response to the events around them. Are they brave, calm, strong and decisive?
- You may also be required to look at the events themselves, and the way they test your chosen hero or heroine. There may be a battle of some kind, or a disaster, or some other situation in which the hero must take charge or sacrifice his own safety for the sake of others. Think about how challenging events can make heroes of the people involved.

> ●●● EXERCISE 3
>
> What sort of acts might be called heroic? Do you know of anyone who has performed an act of heroism? Is it to do with altruism (which means putting others before oneself)?
>
> With a friend, think about the kinds of things people do – in real life and in fiction – that might be regarded as heroic acts. You may wish to think about:
>
> - facing dangers
> - taking risks
> - making sacrifices
> - giving commitments
> - behaving selflessly

ESSAYS

LANGUAGE

- Some of the great stories about famous heroes or heroines – and particularly the great myths and legends – often include descriptive language that is rich and powerful, full of metaphors and similes about *victory*, *courage* and *honour*.
- Such abstract nouns are commonplace in hero stories, and they show the contrast between two opposing sides or concepts, such as *war* and *peace*, *courage* and *cowardice*, *love* and *hate*, or *good* and *evil*.

MORALS AND MESSAGES

- We can often learn a great deal from stories about heroes and heroines. The ways in which these fictional characters face – and overcome – different hardships and challenges; the fact that heroes think of others before themselves; the idea that great men and women still have their weaknesses and no one is perfect, are all recurring messages in books. Think about what authors are trying to tell their readers through the stories and characters they create.
- Similarly there are lessons to be learned by observing what happens to the enemies of literary heroes – seeing the consequences of actions that may be selfish, greedy or unjust. Do the villains get their just desserts?

●●● EXERCISE 4

Working with a partner, see if you can change the endings of these heroic similes and metaphors to create some fresh and exciting ones of your own. Try to keep the same sort of meaning.

- as brave as a lion
- as strong as an ox
- a heart of gold
- a man of steel
- tough as old boots
- sharp as sixpence

●●● EXERCISE 5

In small discussion groups discuss the following questions, giving examples from books you have read wherever you can.

- Do the authors of children's books have a moral responsibility to promote good behaviour over bad?
- Should the heroes always win?
- Can we ever be like the heroes in books?

Model Essay

QUESTION

Choose one or more of your studied texts and, by referring carefully to events which take place, discuss to what extent the central character deserves to be called a hero or heroine.

© *Independent Schools Examinations Board*

Read the following essay, which may be regarded as one way to tackle this question. There are other ways. Remember, in a Common Entrance Examination, you will not be permitted to take your set texts in with you. This means that you may not be expected to quote directly from books. (It is worth checking with your teacher to see if your chosen senior school is expecting you to include direct quotations.) Instead, you will be required to make reference to the events and characters they feature. You will not have much time, so your essay will need to be concise.

Introduction which defines the terms 'hero' and 'heroic', by offering other synonyms.

A hero, or heroine, is someone who is greatly admired for their courage and selflessness. Known for their outstanding achievements, heroes often make sacrifices, like placing themselves at risk so that others may remain safe. To be heroic is to be brave, valiant and just.

For me, one such hero is Captain Stanhope, the central character in R. C. Sheriff's classic war play, Journey's End.

Narrowing focus to a specific hero, giving the character's name and the book involved – answering the question.

Introduce character, before moving on to specific events.

Stanhope is commander of C Company, fighting in the trenches of Northern France during the Great War. The burden of responsibility is heavy, the conditions are appalling, and the future is uncertain, to say the least. Yet Stanhope has 'stuck it out' longer than any man out there. He refuses to take the leave that is due to him, preferring to stay and support his troops, who, in turn, love him.

He spends a great deal of his time on the parapet, alongside his men, 'cheering them on and making them keen on things'. He commands his company with a firm but fair hand. He leads by example. He does not expect his men to do anything he would not do himself.

There are several incidents in the play that highlight his heroic nature. When Hibbert, one of his officers, confesses to feelings of panic and fear at the prospect of spending another day in the trenches, Stanhope's reaction is firm and, at first, uncaring it seems. But he soon shows that he understands what Hibbert is

Several specific examples from the play to highlight Stanhope's heroic nature, and support opening answer.

ESSAYS

going through. He talks to him gently and sympathetically, telling him that he too feels afraid. He persuades him to 'see it through' as they go out into the trenches together.

When the Colonel visits Stanhope's dugout, he gives him the news that his company has been chosen to make a dash across no man's land into enemy lines to retrieve a German soldier for interrogation. Stanhope is told that this must take during the afternoon. He feels that this is entirely the wrong time to carry out the raid, and may endanger the lives of his troops. He questions the wisdom of this decision, but, when the General offers to give the mission to a different company, Stanhope insists that he will carry out the order, knowing that it may carry a yet heavier burden for him as leader. He fears he may be responsible for the deaths of men in his charge, but accepts the responsibility.

> Discussing the significance of each incident, rather than just narrating it.

When the raid is executed, sure enough Stanhope's fears are realised and some of his men do not come back. One of them is Stanhope's second in command, Osborne — a strong and unstinting companion for Stanhope, who 'knows (him) better than anyone out there'. The loss is a very painful one, and Stanhope looks weakened, but nevertheless he presses on, continuing to lead his company and to follow the orders that are given to him, whatever dangers they may bring.

> Exploring how the character feels – showing empathy and understanding

The effects of being at the front line for so long — longer than any other officer — take their toll on Stanhope's health. He drinks and smokes to excess. He seems irrational at times, revealing a short temper and flashes of anger mixed with sorrow. But his courage is never in doubt, and the selfless way he leads his men is impressive, proving that he deserves to be called a hero.

> Quick conclusion to sum up and return to the original question.

●●● EXERCISE 6

Have you read R.C. Sherriff's famous play about life in the trenches of the Great War? Perhaps you have read other plays, stories or poems about war. Can you think of some great people, real or fictional, who may be regarded as war heroes?

Share your knowledge of war heroes with a partner. What sort of characteristics do they have in common?

❓ Essay Questions (Heroes and Heroines)

1 'In order to have a hero, a story must have a villain.' By referring in detail to one or more texts you have studied, discuss to what extent you agree with this view.

2 'One man's hero is another man's enemy.' Discuss this statement, with reference to one or more texts you have studied.

3 Describe the fictional hero you most admire from the texts you have studied.

4 With specific reference to one or more texts you have read, show how authors may broaden the appeal of their fictional heroes by giving them weaknesses as well as strengths.

5 'Heroism is never easy; it requires making some tough decisions.' Discuss your reaction to this statement, referring closely to one or more set texts you have read.

6 'Heroes rarely work alone: their achievements are often the results of partnerships with others.' With reference to one or more texts you have studied, discuss to what extent you think this is true.

7 We can all feel heroic when times are good, but a true hero emerges when the going gets tough. By referring closely to one or more texts you have studied, show how authors test their fictional heroes by placing them in difficulty.

↔ Extended Writing Questions

8 Write a discussion piece entitled 'What you need to be a hero'. In your essay discuss the various attributes we might expect a true hero to possess and the kinds of actions that might be considered to be heroic deeds.

9 Choose two different fictional heroes from two separate books you have read. Compare and contrast these heroic characters in an essay, looking at their characteristics, actions, reputations, successes and failures. State in your conclusion which of the two characters you consider to be the greater hero, and why.

10 Write an excerpt from an imaginary story which explores the loneliness and isolation a war hero may feel when he or she returns home. Upon his (or her) return, the hero is surprised to find that he no longer gains the respect of ordinary civilians who fail to understand what he has been through.

📖 Wider Reading

11 Read Philip Pullman's *Northern Lights*. Consider to what extent Lyra might be considered a heroine. Does she possess the right characteristics? Try to support your comments and observations with specific examples from the story.

12 The following works of fiction explore the theme of Heroes and Heroines:
- *Journey's End* by R.C. Sherriff (Penguin, 2000)
- *Lord of the Flies* by William Golding (Faber and Faber, 1997)
- *Smith* by Leon Garfield (Puffin, 1994)
- *Northern Lights* by Phillip Pullman (Scholastic, 2005)
- *The Dolphin Crossing* by Jill Paton Walsh (Puffin, 1970)
- *Goodnight Mister Tom* by Michelle Magorian (Puffin, 1983)
- *The Lord of the Rings* by J.R.R. Tolkien (HarperCollins, 2005)
- *Stormbreaker* by Anthony Horowitz (Walker Books, 2005)
- *The Hound of the Baskervilles* by Arthur Conan Doyle (Penguin, 1996)

You may also like to read the well-known true story about living through war, by Anne Frank, entitled *The Diary of Anne Frank* (Imprint, 1989).

ESSAYS

4.4 Conflict

 Discussion

Conflict means serious disagreement. It can result in arguments, broken friendships, fights and even wars. In fiction, when two sides come into conflict a drama is created – around which a story may be built.

The dramatic tension in many stories is derived from a conflict of some kind. It is, after all, more interesting to read about how conflicting characters try to resolve their differences, than simply how much they like one another. Stories would be dull if their characters were in agreement all of the time. As readers we are invited to decide who is right, who is wrong, how the conflicts arose, and how best they can be resolved.

Conflict in literature reflects the conflicts that, sadly, we see around us in our everyday lives.

You will find many of these 'flashpoints' in literature, as authors try to create realistic characters, with their own individual views and beliefs.

The questions to consider are: How do authors create convincing conflicts, and how do they use conflict to bring their characters – and their stories – to life?

 Focus

CHARACTERS

- For stories to really capture our interest, they need to offer us characters that differ in many ways. Just as in real life different people sometimes hold different opinions, so in stories the fictional characters may respond differently to the circumstances they are in. Think about how the characters differ – focus on their experiences, beliefs and values.
- When conflict arises in a story, soon two sides will emerge, both of which may consider themselves right. Some characters may be stubborn, others more flexible, some will be trying to work for a compromise, while others may be plotting an attack. Which characters will you sympathise with?

● ● ● EXERCISE 1

Why do people fall out? How does conflict arise? What are the 'flashpoints' in life that sometimes cause serious disagreement?

Working with a partner, make a list of some controversial issues that can sometimes lead to conflict between people. You could begin with: *money*.

Share your ideas with the class.

● ● ● EXERCISE 2

Can you think of stories that involve some kind of conflict? (Almost all stories do!).

Choose one or two fictional conflicts, then write down one character from each side. List some reasons they may have for believing they are right (and the others are wrong).

ACTIONS AND EVENTS

- Just as in real life, when serious disagreement takes places between fictional characters, it will influence their actions and the events that unfold. There may be plots, schemes and conspiracies. There may be meetings, debates or even battles. When studying this theme, consider how each conflict shapes the plot and influences the characters' actions.

- Whether it arises within families and relationships, in society, or even between countries, conflict can often escalate. Think about how one small disagreement may lead to more serious disputes – and then consider what readers can learn from the actions of those involved. Can there be winners as well as losers?

LANGUAGE

- When conflicts arise in stories, authors will use language carefully to build tension and highlight characters' emotions as the conflict escalates. Often metaphors and similes will be used to describe tense moments (e.g. *the atmosphere in the room chilled* or *silence fell like a dark cloak*). Likewise the reactions of characters may be equally dramatic (*he exploded in rage* or *her stare was as cold as ice*).

- Stories with conflicts may be narrated in either first or third person narrative. Whichever is used, the frustration, anger or pain felt by the characters involved will be described in detail – right down to their facial expressions and the tone of their voice – in order to engage readers in the drama as it unfolds.

●●● EXERCISE 3

What are the best ways of solving disputes and avoiding serious conflict?

With a friend, write down a short guide to help people prevent small disagreements from escalating into major conflicts.

You may want to think about:

- the importance of talking to one another
- why we should be tolerant
- how not to lose sight of what's important
- keeping a sense of proportion and perspective

●●● EXERCISE 4

Think back to a time when you found yourself in serious disagreement with someone – perhaps a playground dispute, or a battle about when you should go to bed (or get up!).

What was the atmosphere like in the room? Write a few sentences to describe the atmosphere during one such argument. Use similes and metaphors. You may like to think about:

- temperature
- sound
- movement
- facial expressions
- voice tones

Share your sentences with a partner.

MORALS AND MESSAGES

- Usually, though not always, the conflicts in stories become resolved in some way. Grievances may be forgotten, harsh words forgiven and wounds healed. This is because most readers like happy endings. However, sometimes solutions are not as easily found. In most cases, fictional conflicts usually carry some form of message for the reader, e.g. keep talking, don't hold grudges, play fair, work hard, tolerate one another's differences, and so on.
- When studying conflict in novels, try to identify the moral of the story – what the author wishes to say to readers through the conflict and its consequences.

> ● ● ● **EXERCISE 5**
>
> Working in small groups, think of some of the books you have read that involve conflicts of some kind – these may be war stories, human interest stories about family and growing up, or perhaps science-fiction and fantasy.
>
> In each case, discuss together any lessons that can be learned from watching conflict affect people's lives, and seeing how it can be avoided.

📖 Model Essay

QUESTION

The rule of law is usually enforced to stop conflict, but sometimes it can increase it. Referring to one or two texts you have studied, show how writers deal with the operation of rules or the law.

© Independent Schools Examinations Board

Here is one way to tackle this challenging question. You may think of other texts and have many other comments to make.

Look at the structure of the essay, the order it follows and the important features that have been highlighted.

Introduction to show you understand the question.	*Laws are established to prevent conflict from arising, and to provide a fair and just outcome when people are unable to sort out their differences for themselves. Theoretically if people abide by the rule of law, then conflicts should not arise.*	
	However, even when laws are made democratically, there will be those in the minority for whom a law may be deeply unpopular. Some may even refuse to abide by them.	Offer reasons why laws can increase conflict rather than prevent it.

Introduce the chosen text and explain why it is an appropriate choice.

Few stories highlight the controversial nature of law-making more than William Golding's Lord of the Flies. In this story, an aeroplane carrying young evacuees crash-lands on a remote island. The air crew are killed in the crash, leaving the young children – all boys – to fend for themselves.

In the absence of 'grown ups', and far away from the strict orderliness that once ruled their lives, the children are free to live as they choose.

Set the context/ give brief synopsis of story before discussing specific questions.

At first, the boys' time is spent playing games and getting up to mischief. But soon they realise that in order to survive and be rescued, they must establish a sense of law and order on the island. There is food to be gathered, shelters to be made and a fire must be kept alight to attract rescuers to the island.

A conch shell is used in circle meetings to give individuals a chance to speak and, since he was the one who found it, Ralph is elected leader of the group. Jack Merridew, a domineering head chorister is given the choir as hunters. Rules are established that should ensure fair play and the survival of everyone.

Discuss examples of laws increasing conflict rather than preventing it on the island.

However, as in real life, not all the laws are popular with all the people. Jack, who resents Ralph's authority and sees it as a threat to his own freedom, begins to flout the rules. He and his gang of hunters fail to keep the fire going, missing a precious opportunity to attract the attention of a passing ship. He refuses to build shelters, preferring to establish his own 'castle' at the other end of the island. He denies Piggy's right to his pair of spectacles – an essential tool for fire-lighting and a symbol of authority and power. And he even holds ritualistic dances around the camp fire, which lead to the eventual murder of Simon, whom they mistake for the 'beast'.

In many ways, the laws which were established on the island, and were designed to prevent conflict and disorder, had the reverse effect, causing resentment, rebellion and the eventual slide into savagery.

Return to the question again, to keep on track and stay relevant.

Conclude by sharing what Golding teaches us in the way he deals with law and order in his story.

Golding deals with the operation of law and order by showing us what can happen when rules, which are established by a majority, are flouted by a minority. When the conch, which comes to symbolise justice and order in the story, is smashed into tiny fragments, this reminds us how fragile such a system of democratic rule really is. When one person can persuade many others not to abide by the laws laid down, order descends into chaos and, as Golding demonstrates, this then turns into a much more brutal system of ruling, through fear and oppression.

In *Lord of the Flies*, children find themselves alone on an island with no adults, and no rules to have to obey. How do you think you would cope – would you enjoy having no rules, or do you believe that rules are necessary?

Share your views with a partner. If you know the story, discuss which character you think you might be!

? Essay Questions (Conflict)

1   'When major conflict strikes, there are rarely any winners, only losers.' Discuss to what extent you agree with this statement, referring to one or more texts you have read by way of examples.

2   By referring to one or more stories you have read, show how small arguments can escalate into major conflicts when people stop talking and listening to one another.

3   The theme of conflict can bring drama and suspense to a story. Illustrate this by referring to one or more texts you have read.

4   Sometimes people can become so caught up in conflicts with others that they lose the ability to think rationally or behave sensibly. Give one or more examples of fictional characters becoming caught up in conflict in this way.

5   'A true leader must face and overcome conflict before he or she may be considered worthy of other people's respect.' Comment on how far this has been true in the stories you have read.

6   Conflicts can sometimes arise between people of different ages, with different life experiences and different values. Referring to one or more texts you have read, show how authors explore the tensions that can exist between younger and older generations.

7   Referring to one or more texts you have studied, show how conflict can be overcome through tolerance, empathy and honest dialogue.

↔ Extended Writing Questions

8   Write an excerpt from a fictional diary in which you are caught up in a conflict of some kind. Describe your feelings and thoughts in response to the difficult situation you are in.

9   Write a speech for or against the use of military force to solve international conflicts. Discuss the advantages, or disadvantages, of more peaceful methods.

10   Think of a story you have read that involves a conflict of some kind. Take two characters from the story – one from each of the opposing sides – and write a play script in which they try to convince each other that their own opinion is the correct one.

📖 Wider Reading

11   Read George Orwell's famous story, *Animal Farm*. Write an essay in which you explain why the pigs' leadership of the farm leads to yet more conflict on the farm, after Jones is ousted in the rebellion.

12   The following texts explore the theme of Conflict:

- *Noughts and Crosses* by Malorie Blackman (Corgi Children's, 2002)
- *A Kestrel for a Knave* by Barry Hines (Penguin, 2000)
- *War of Jenkin's Ear* by Michael Morpurgo (Heinemann Young Books, 1993)
- *You Don't Know Me* by David Klass (Viking, 2001)
- *The Curious Incident of the Dog in the Night-time* by Mark Haddon (Red Fox, 2004)
- *Animal Farm* by George Orwell (Penguin, 1996)
- *1984* by George Orwell (Penguin, 1990)
- *Journey's End* by R.C. Sherriff (Penguin, 2000)
- *Lord of the Flies* by William Golding (Faber and Faber, 1997)
- *The Dolphin Crossing* by Jill Paton Walsh (Puffin, 1970)

4.5 Freedom

Discussion

'Freedom', and its opposite, 'oppression or imprisonment', are themes that are often explored in stories. To have freedom is, after all, a precious gift to be given, and yet one which many of us may take for granted.

As a literary theme, freedom may come in various forms: a prisoner being set free after years of imprisonment, a country being released from a brutal dictator, a wild animal escaping a zoo, even a school pupil experiencing the joys of the summer holiday after a long year in the classroom!

When reading texts that explore this theme, consider how the freedom improves the lives of the characters involved – and what their lives might be like without it.

Freedom is one of the most cherished things most of us have in life – and it is something that many people would fight for – even die for.

Some of the most dramatic stories describe the effects on the human spirit when a person's freedom is taken away. Years of imprisonment or oppression can take their toll on a person's mind, particularly when hope slowly fades away...

●●● EXERCISE 1

Can you think of other ways in which fictional characters in stories may feel a sense of freedom?

Working in small groups, make a list of ways in which freedom might be introduced in a story. You could begin with the forms of freedom referred to in the Discussion section.

Focus

CHARACTERS

- In stories about freedom and oppression, authors will often focus in detail on the way in which freedom, or the lack of it, impacts on the lives of one or two particular characters. Even when a whole nation is denied its freedom, focusing on just one or two personal stories can highlight the personal consequences for its people.

- When people lose their freedom, there may be a whole range of different spirits and personalities that emerge, from courageous optimists, to weak and defeated spirits, from determined activists, hell-bent on escape, to leaders who try to make the best of what little they are given.

ACTIONS AND EVENTS

- In stories that explore the theme of freedom, there may be actions and events within the plot that lead to imprisonment or oppression. These could include: a hostage being taken; a brutal tyrant invading a country; a crime being committed which leads to a case of mistaken identity and wrongful imprisonment; even an accident which robs someone of their independence.

- In such stories, the rest of the plot may be shaped by the characters' plans to regain their freedom in some way, and this might include:
  - military action
  - jail breaks
  - appeals against laws and rulings
  - a process of rehabilitation and adjustment
  - coming to terms with a loss of personal freedom, through illness or accident.

●●● EXERCISE 2

If you were caught up in a situation in which you were denied your freedom for a period of time, which type of person would you become? Would you organise a plot to escape and risk the consequences? Would you try to ride it out and make the best of what you've got? Would you cry and moan, or would you remain quietly determined?

Discuss with a friend how you might react in such a situation.

●●● EXERCISE 3

Working in small writing groups, see if you can come up with an original plot for a new story about freedom.

Choose one of the major events suggested to the left. Then put several smaller events on a story timeline, showing what happens leading up to, and following on from, the removal of someone's freedom. You could choose a wrongful imprisonment and then a jail break or an appeal trial in which the character is then acquitted...

LANGUAGE

- In stories about freedom, authors will use interesting adjectives to convey the feelings of those characters who may have lost – or regained – their freedom. Adjectives may range from: *isolated, worthless* and *confined*, to *liberated, reborn* and *sanguine*.
- When trying to convey these feelings, authors may also use figurative language (e.g. metaphors and similes) to accentuate the effects of being imprisoned or the feeling of being set free, for example, *caught like a snared rabbit* or *free to take flight at last*.

MORALS AND MESSAGES

- The obvious lesson which we may learn from stories about freedom is not to take our own liberty for granted. There are many stories that tell of others less fortunate than ourselves who must endure a life fenced in by restrictions of one kind or another. Consider how each author highlights the value of freedom by taking it away from one or more of their own characters – and then describing the effects.
- In real life, people are sometimes willing to sacrifice their own freedom for the sake of justice or the liberty of others – and the same is true in fictional stories. In these cases, consider what drives the brave people who speak up – what are they fighting for and why are they willing to be locked up for what they believe?

●●● EXERCISE 4

How might you feel if you were robbed of your freedom? Have you ever been kept in at break time?! How did you feel?

Working closely with a partner, make two lists of words: the first will contain adjectives that accurately convey your feelings, as you sit inside a classroom at break time, watching your friends playing outside; the other will show words that describe your feelings the moment the bell rings and the doors open to signal the end of school!

You could begin with:

Kept in	Let out
frustrated	animated
caged in	energised
worthless	unrestricted

●●● EXERCISE 5

Consider the extraordinary life of Nelson Mandela, the former prisoner held in a South African jail for speaking out against the racial division and oppression in his homeland. Twenty-seven years later, upon his release, he became president of his country.

Share what you know about Mandela. Find out more, if you can, from books, websites and encyclopaedias.

ESSAYS

Model Essay

QUESTION

Recommend a story you have read which taught you important lessons about the real value of freedom.

Read the following essay, which may be regarded as one way to tackle this question. There are other ways. Remember, in a Common Entrance Examination, you will not be permitted to take your set texts in with you. This means that you are not expected to quote directly from books, although if quotations occur to you, you may include them. Instead, you will be required to make reference to the events and characters they feature. You will not have much time, so your essay will need to be concise.

> Opening sentences to set the context and show you are on the right track.

Some stories can teach us valuable lessons about how important our freedom is. They can show us how we might feel when it is taken away from us and we are left trapped, like a caged animal, with no rights or privileges.

One story that taught me to appreciate my own freedom is 'Amongst the Hidden' by Margaret Haddix.

> Introduce the story you would like to recommend, and set the scene.

In this story, Luke Garner lives what looks, at first, like a normal life, as the third child of Mr and Mrs Garner, in a normal house in an average part of town. But Luke has a secret – in fact Luke is a secret. For the Government has passed a law forbidding parents to have any more than two children. If the Population Police find a third child, he or she will be removed from the families and locked away, or worse...

> Further explanations of the role of freedom in your chosen book.

Consequently, Luke must spend his life peering out at passers-by from behind the shuttered windows of his home. Life is made much worse at the beginning of the story, when news comes that the woods behind his house are to be cleared to make way for a new housing estate. This means that his garden – which until now has been secluded, hidden from prying eyes and therefore a safe place for Luke to experience the fresh, open air – will soon become overlooked from every direction and therefore out of bounds to him. His imprisonment inside his own house is complete.

Throughout the story there are times when I am reminded how much I may take my own freedom for granted. The freedom to go shopping for example, or make new friends at school, or visit the cinema, or just walk down the street in daylight.

> Show how the book affects you – and why you would recommend it.

Luke's brothers are safe to enjoy such pursuits, and this helps to emphasise the restrictions placed on Luke's own life. In some ways, I feel like one of Luke's brothers, watching closely what happens to Luke, sharing his thoughts and feelings, but then able to come and go as I please.

One day, Luke makes an extraordinary discovery. While peeking out between the vents in the wall of his attic room, he notices something through the window of the Sports family opposite. It is a pair of eyes peering back at him – in a house where two children already lived, and they were all out.

Luke soon befriends Jen, a third child too, but very different in nature. Jen refuses to accept her fate. She rejects the Population Law and will not rest until she has changed the system in some way, so that she, and all other third children, may be treated as free human beings, like their more fortunate siblings.

> Try to keep your story narration concise and relevant.

Communicating is very difficult for Luke and Jen, as one might expect. Luke even has to count – and memorise – the number of people who come and go in his street everyday, so that he knows when it is safe to run across the road to see his new friend. If any neighbour saw him they would be bound to turn him in to the Population Police.

There is one poignant moment, as he dashed across the road, when we are told that Luke had 'forgotten what fresh air felt like'.

> Further confirmation of how book teaches you to appreciate your own freedom (i.e. answering the question).

When in the company of Jen, Luke (and the reader) learn of the ways in which Jen intends to 'fight for her freedom' – a freedom that, in real life, we enjoy without question. Such a fight ends tragically for Jen – she is shot by the authorities as she attends a protest march past the president's house.

> Concluding paragraphs to sum up how it affects you and why you would recommend it to others.

I strongly recommend readers to read this story, which is an exciting adventure, as well as a thought-provoking tale of oppression, injustice and imprisonment. Once you have read it, you will not fail to appreciate how free you really are.

●●● EXERCISE 6

Working in small discussion groups, share your thoughts about what you would miss most if, like Luke Garner, you were forced to live in the shadows, unable even to leave your own house.

Then listen, and respond to, the views of others in your class. Are there some things that many of you would miss?

Is it hard to imagine, because we all take our freedom for granted anyway?

❓ Essay Questions (Freedom)

1 'Freedom is a right rather than a privilege.' Comment on the extent to which you agree with this statement, citing one or more examples from books you have read which show the effects caused when freedom is taken away from someone.

2 With reference to one or more stories you have read, describe a fictional character who clings to the freedom of their imagination whilst being physically trapped, through disability or imprisonment.

3 Like many good things in life, one never appreciates one's own freedom until it is taken away. With reference to one or more fictional texts, illustrate how authors show the value of freedom, and how we should not take it for granted in case we lose it one day.

4 Some children strive to be free to do the things that grown ups can do. Then, when they are older, they wish they were children again, free from the stresses and strains that come with being a responsible adult. Describe a fictional character you are familiar with, for whom this is particularly true.

5 In modern Britain, people of all races are free to do what they want to do, within the law. But in other countries, even today, some racial minorities are less fortunate. Refer to the lessons you have learned from one or more texts you have read in which people of a particular race are trapped by the prejudice of others.

6 What must it feel like to regain one's freedom again, after years of imprisonment or oppression? Citing one or more examples from books you have read, describe the feelings of a fictional character(s) who is given their liberty again, after living without it for a long period.

7 Animals have as much of a right to freedom as humans. Using one or more examples from books you have read, describe the harmful effects caused to animals when their freedom is taken away.

↔ Extended Writing Questions

8 Write an essay discussing different views concerning the keeping of animals in captivity. Do zoos and safari parks play an important role in breeding programmes and protecting species from extinction, or should all exotic animals enjoy the freedom to roam in the wild?

9 Write a page or two from the imaginary diary of a prisoner, wrongfully imprisoned for a crime that he or she did not commit.

10 Write a story in which a caged animal is set free, to return to its rightful home in the wild. Compare and contrast the animal's response to being in captivity with its first reactions to being back in the wide open spaces of its natural habitat. You may like to choose a grizzly bear, an orang-utan, or perhaps a dolphin, for example.

📖 Wider Reading

11 George Orwell's classic work of fiction, *Animal Farm*, explores the themes of conflict *and* freedom. Read the story and then write an essay discussing the reasons why the animals rebelled against their oppressor, Mr Jones, in the first place, and whether their new-found freedom under the pigs is any better.

12 These texts explore the theme of Freedom:
- *Amongst the Hidden* (Red Fox, 2001), *Running out of Time* (Definitions, 2001) and *Amongst the Imposters* (Red Fox, 2001) – series by Margaret Haddix
- *To Kill a Mockingbird* by Harper Lee (Vintage, 2004)
- *The Snow Goose* by Paul Gallico (Longman, 2000)
- *Tuck Everlasting* by Natalie Babbitt (Bloomsbury, 2003)
- *Lord of the Flies* by William Golding (Faber and Faber, 1997)
- *Animal Farm* by George Orwell (Penguin, 1996)
- *1984* by George Orwell (Penguin, 1990)
- *The Man in the Iron Mask* by Alexandre Dumas (Penguin, 2003)

4.6 Ambition

 ## Discussion

The Oxford English Dictionary (2004) defines ambition as 'a strong desire to do or achieve something'.

Whether it is a desire for wealth, happiness, power or fame – or even all four – most of us harbour one kind of ambition or another. It is what motivates us.

By giving their fictional characters ambitions, authors broaden their appeal, enabling readers to identify with them, perhaps even sympathise. Finding out whether characters actually achieve their goals always makes a good story.

The questions in Exercise 1 are big questions – ones which we all ask ourselves from time to time. So it is interesting to see how characters in stories get on, as they strive to realise their own goals. We may even learn something along the way.

> ### ●●● EXERCISE 1
>
> What sort of ambitions do you have? With a friend, discuss the questions below. You can be as honest as you choose to be!
>
> - What do you hope to achieve in school?
> - What would you like to do when you are older?
> - How do you think you will find happiness?
> - Is wealth important to you?
> - What motivates you to get up in the morning?

 ## Focus

CHARACTERS

- It is what ambition can do to people that makes this theme such a compelling one for authors to explore in stories. For some, ambition can become an addiction, influencing the way they live their lives and preventing them from ever finding contentment. The frustration which characters may feel when their goals seem so far away, may lead to resentment and animosity – and this makes for good drama in stories!
- Some fictional characters – just like the one featured in the sample essay below – show us what can happen when we allow ambition alone to rule our lives.
- In other situations, the determination, courage and resilience that a character needs to fulfil his or her ambition often makes for a very interesting – and inspiring – story.

> ### ●●● EXERCISE 2
>
> Working in small discussion groups, think of some stories you have read recently in which characters have had dreams or ambitions which they have tried to fulfil. Did they manage it? Were they always happy along the way? How did their ambitions or goals affect the way they felt?
>
> The following table shows some of the positive and negative qualities that ambitious characters may feel in stories. Copy it out and see if you can add more.
>
> | Positive qualities: | Negative qualities |
> | --- | --- |
> | focused | nervous |
> | excited | obsessed |
> | driven | discontented |

ACTIONS AND EVENTS

- The goals and ambitions that characters may have – and the all important 'journeys' they must make to realise these goals – provide storywriters with ample material to construct an interesting story plot. As you read stories on this theme, try to identify the direction in which the plot is heading. Which events are crucial to the plot, and which are distractions?
- When thinking about characters' actions, consider the following questions:
  - To what extent do the ambitions of characters affect the way they behave and interact with others in the story?
  - Can you see their frustrations building?
  - Can you sympathise with them?
  - Would you act in the same way if it were you?

LANGUAGE

- Often we talk of our ambitions and goals as 'mountains to climb' or 'long journeys to make', meaning there is a lot we must do in order to arrive at the place we should like to be in life. In stories, authors often use these and other metaphors and similes to describe the ambitions and goals of their fictional characters.
- Similarly, ambition itself is often spoken of in ways which personify it – that is to say it is treated as a person or force in its own right, and this can have an impact on those who hold ambition in their heads, for example, *ambition was eating away at his mind* or *it was her ambition that spurred her on*.

MORALS AND MESSAGES

- Ambition can be a motivating force for us all, but it can also lead to unhappiness, particularly if the goals we set ourselves are just too difficult, or they stem from selfishness and greed. This is one of the lessons we can learn from stories about ambition.
- Similarly, when fictional characters achieve the goals they set themselves we can learn a lot by seeing how their determination and courage won in the end. Our challenges in real life may be different from the quests faced by our favourite storybook characters, but the qualities needed to achieve success may be the same.

●●● EXERCISE 3

Choose one ambition from the list below. Then think of some possible steps or hurdles that may arise along the road to achieving this ambition. Sketch out a quick story plot or timeline, based on this ambition, showing the kinds of events – good and bad – along the way.

- climbing Mount Everest
- becoming Prime Minister
- making a million pounds
- creating a world famous sculpture
- writing a best-selling book

●●● EXERCISE 4

With a partner, think of the goals and ambitions you have. How might you describe your journey to reach them – as a steep climb, a long, winding road, or perhaps a race that must be won?

See if you can come up with some fresh metaphors for the challenges you set yourself in life.

Working with a partner, think of two different examples of ambitious characters in stories you have read – one where ambition has brought happiness and success; the other in which ambition brings greed and unhappiness.

Can you identify what went wrong/right?

 # Model Essay

QUESTION

Referring to one or more texts you have studied, illustrate how ambition can lead to greed and unhappiness in life.

Read the following essay, which may be regarded as one way to tackle this question. There are other ways. Remember, in a Common Entrance Examination, you will not be permitted to take your set texts in with you. You may be able to learn some quotations on the theme of ambition from the books you have read, otherwise try to make reference to the events and characters they feature.

> | Introduction to show you know what *ambition* means. |

Ambition is a strong desire to do, or achieve, something great. It can be a positive driving force for many people, but it can also bring unhappiness and greed if it is allowed to rule someone's life. Ambition can become an addiction that must always be satisfied, whatever the cost.

An illustration of how ambition can become a fatal weakness may be seen clearly in the rise and fall of the fictional character Macbeth, in William Shakespeare's famous play of the same name. The story begins with Macbeth being celebrated as a brave war hero, a noble and loyal subject of Duncan, the Scottish king. It ends with Macbeth meeting his fate for the murderous crimes he has committed, including the savage and brutal murders of both Duncan and his own trusted friend, Banquo. It could be argued that it is ambition and ultimately greed that leads Macbeth into this deathly decline.

It is the witches that Macbeth meets on the heath that are the architects of Macbeth's downfall. It is they who plant the seeds of power in his mind, turning ambition into greed. He is told that he shall become 'Thane of Cawdor', and 'king thereafter'. Sure enough, when Duncan hears of his valiant efforts in quashing the rebels, he rewards him with the title Thane of Cawdor. Thus the first of the witches' prophecies has come true.

> | Choose a character that will illustrate the point of the question. |

ESSAYS

Quick synopsis of play, focusing on ambition of lead character throughout.

When Macbeth shares the news of his strange encounter on the heath with his wife, Lady Macbeth, she convinces him that there may have been truth in what the witches said, and that Macbeth is indeed destined to become king of Scotland. This fuels his ambition yet further. He becomes focused on his goal, no longer able to think rationally. When Duncan is invited to stay with Macbeth and his wife, his host seizes his chance to turn his ambitions into reality. With the help and constant reassurance of his wife — whose own ambition is all-consuming — he commits regicide. Duncan's sons flee, afraid that they will be blamed for his murder, and Macbeth is crowned king.

The ambition to become king has, it seems, been fulfilled. But the witches had made a third prophesy, which was that his loyal friend Banquo would be the father of kings. This troubles Macbeth greatly, believing that this third prediction might jeopardise his position. It is his ambition to remain safely on the throne that leads him to commit his second murderous act — to arrange for Banquo to be killed whilst out riding. Although Fleance, Banquo's son, escapes, Banquo lies silenced in a ditch.

Highlight the consequences when ambition turns to greed.

The play ends with Macbeth meeting his fate at the hands of Macduff, whose own family is killed at Macbeth's request — a warning shot to Macduff to stay clear of him.

Return to the question and answer it as part of the conclusion.

The tragic story of Macbeth illustrates how ambition can lead to greed and unhappiness. Macbeth is greedy for power. He will never be happy until he feels that his position as king is unthreatened — an ambition which can never be achieved, given the circumstances in which he is crowned.

Though the witches and his evil wife encourage him to control his own fate, it is his own ambition, that was already present within him, that ultimately makes him vulnerable to suggestion and greedy for power. His ambition had been allowed to consume his life, and the lives of those around him.

●●● EXERCISE 6

Have you read or seen a performance of Shakespeare's *Macbeth*? Do you recognise the characters mentioned here?

Can you think of another example from a story or play you have read in which ambition becomes a force for evil rather than a force for good?

Share your ideas with a friend.

? Essay Questions (Ambition)

1 Which is better, to have ambitions but never fulfil them, or to have no ambitions at all? Address this question by referring to examples of ambitious or unambitious characters in one or more texts you have studied.

2 'Racing to fulfil an ambition rarely ends in success. It is all about pacing and planning.' Give a response to this statement, with reference to some examples from one or more texts you have studied.

3 Share one or more examples, from set texts you have studied, of a character fulfilling a lifetime's ambition.

4 'Ambitious people are never satisfied.' Discuss this statement giving examples from one or more texts you have studied.

5 'When people become too ambitious, they forget the needs of others around them.' Discuss whether you think is true, using examples from one or more texts you have studied.

6 Referring to one or more texts you have studied, discuss how you have been inspired by the achievements of others in fulfilling their ambitions.

7 Without ambition, we may never have bettered ourselves and prospered as a country. Using at least one fictional or non-fictional text you have read, show how ambitious individuals have helped to make this country what it is today.

↔ Extended Writing Questions

8 Write about an ambition that you held for a long time, which has now been fulfilled. It may involve sport, like getting into the first XI cricket team, or it may be a musical ambition, like playing first violin in an orchestra. Describe the hard work and commitment needed to reach your goal, and the happiness and pride you felt once the ambition was realised.

9 Imagine you are one of the fictional (or non-fictional) characters you have read about in a book or story which involves a great ambition of some kind. You have been asked to write a letter to all the children out there who would like to follow in your footsteps. What advice will you give about how to reach your goals?

10 Is it good to have great ambitions? Does it depend on what it is you are striving for? Can some ambitions be judged more worthwhile than others (e.g. to build a million-pound business/to establish a charity/to live a sustainable, eco-friendly life/to win the lottery)? Write a discursive essay on the pros and cons of having ambitions.

📖 Wider Reading

11 Read Paulo Coelho's international bestseller, *The Alchemist*. Write an essay sharing your thoughts about what this simple story can teach us about our ambitions in life.

12 The following texts explore the theme of Ambition:
   - *Macbeth* by William Shakespeare (Penguin, 1994)
   - *The Time Machine* by H.G. Wells (Penguin, 2005)
   - *Treasure Island* by Robert Louis Stevenson (Puffin, 1994)
   - *Journey to the Centre of the Earth* by Jules Verne (Penguin, 1994)
   - *The Alchemist* by Paulo Coelho (HarperCollins, 1999)
   - *Lord of the Rings* by J.R.R. Tolkien (HarperCollins, 2005)
   - *The Dolphin Crossing* by Jill Paton Walsh (Puffin, 1970)
   - *Great Expectations* by Charles Dickens (Penguin, 2007)
   - *Coram Boy* by Jamila Gavin (Egmont, 2004)
   - *Death of a Salesman* by Arthur Miller (Heinemann Educational, 1994)

ESSAYS

UNIT 5
WRITING COMPOSITIONS

INTRODUCTION

Examination requirements

In this unit you will develop the skills needed to tackle the second section of the writing paper for Common Entrance, entitled 'Response to Writing Task'.

In this section of the examination you will be given six optional questions, from which you must choose just one. Each question offers you the chance to write in a different genre. The range may include (but will not be limited to) the following kinds of writing:

- descriptive
- discursive
- personal
- persuasive
- narrative

These terms are explained in turn throughout this unit. There are many differences between these genres in terms of audience, purpose, structure, language features and so on, but your objectives will be the same whichever question you choose to answer. You will need to:

- interpret the question in an interesting and original way
- use grammar, spelling and punctuation as accurately as you can
- attract – and hold – your reader's attention through exciting use of language and literary techniques
- strive for both quality and quantity at all times

Good writing is not only well-presented and accurate, it is creative, dynamic, vibrant and distinctive. Originality and flair will always be rewarded.

The amount of time available in the exam for you to produce writing of such quality is very limited: 40 minutes, including planning time! But your task is not an impossible one, provided you focus on your objectives, keep a clear head and remember to choose a task that inspires you.

Range of genres (choosing the right question)

As explained in the introduction, in the Common Entrance Paper 2 you will be required to answer one question from a range of options, which is likely to include: descriptive, discursive, personal, persuasive and narrative writing. So which one should you choose? The answer, of course, is choose the genre that best suits your style of writing and inspires you the most.

Some questions may seem more attractive to you than others; we all have our favourite kinds of text that we like to read or write. But it is important not to specialise too much in one particular type of writing – just in case it does not appear as an option in the final exam.

> ●●● EXERCISE 1
>
> In small groups, share your views on the kinds of writing you like to do. Which kinds do you think you are good at?
>
> Try to give reasons to support the answers you give. Is the kind of writing you like to do affected by what you like to read? Why should that be?

Luckily there are enough writing options in the examination to keep most people happy! It is very important to remember that you must only choose **one** question and answer it fully – with a page or two of writing. Do NOT attempt to answer every question in 40 minutes.

The range of writing tasks usually offered in Paper 2 is discussed in more detail in this unit, each genre is explored and sample questions are offered. As you learn more about each one, decide for yourself whether it is a genre that inspires you and raises possible ideas and interpretations in your mind.

PLANNING

Ideas and interpretations

The hardest part of any writing exam is choosing the question and then thinking of ideas. After all, most people feel nervous and rushed during exams – feelings which are unlikely to lead to flashes of inspiration and creative thought!

For the more directed questions – like a debate speech on a particular motion, for example – there will be less need for creative inspiration and more demand for focused and incisive writing. But for other, more open-ended questions, like a story title, or a given line which must be included or a place to be described, you may find yourself scratching your head for inspiration.

Choose anything. Take the plunge. Occasionally you may gain marks for an incredibly original and inspired idea, but what matters just as much is *how* you write, for example:

- the accuracy of your grammar and spelling
- the range of your vocabulary
- the richness of your descriptive language

Similarly, it is not necessary to interpret questions in a unique and clever fashion. Interesting ways of interpreting a title may occur to you: 'The Climb', for example, could be taken as a metaphor for striving to get into the 1st XI in cricket, or perhaps the long road to passing CE. However, it is perfectly acceptable to choose a more obvious idea – in this case, a story about a mountain expedition. The most important thing is to select your question quickly, choose the first reasonable idea that comes to you... and then get writing!

> ● ● ● EXERCISE 2
>
> In pairs, discuss each of the following titles, which you might find in a Common Entrance English Paper 2. Talk about what each title makes you think of. How could you interpret it? Will it be a story, a personal account or an essay, for example?
>
> - Guilty as Charged
> - My Greatest Challenge
> - Victory at a Price
> - Building Bridges
> - An Unpleasant Surprise
> - Freedom

Making notes

Once you have chosen your question, decided how you are going to interpret it, and then allowed some creative ideas to take shape in your head, you need to make a few planning notes on paper. You will not have much time to write your composition so do not spend any more than **three minutes** planning it.

If your composition is to be a short story (or an excerpt from an imaginary story that you might write if you had more time) then some brief references to **plot**, **characters** and **setting** would be useful. Set these out in bullet points or as part of a mind-map or spidergram. If, on the other hand, you choose to write about something that happened to you in your own life (personal writing), then jot down the **time**, the **place** and some words and phrases to jog your recollection of the particular incident.

Your planning work will not be collected in – but it will help you by giving your writing a focus and a sense of direction. Do NOT begin writing a 'first draft' of your composition in rough; this is not the aim of planning, which is more about organising your thoughts and looking ahead, rather than rehearsing what you will say.

DRAFTING

Getting started

Once you have thought about how you might develop your idea – and made a few bullet points to guide your thinking – it's time to get started. The opening paragraph is very important – it is what will make you stand out from the dozens of other students whose scripts the examiner will be marking.

Whether you choose to write a story excerpt, a speech, or some personal writing, you will still need to make a positive impact from the beginning, so choose **exciting language** that engages the reader and makes them curious to know more.

During the course of this unit, you will see lots of interesting ways to begin each of the different genres that feature in the exam.

Remember: you need to create a good impression in your first paragraph. This can be achieved through:

- accurate spelling and grammar
- exciting language
- interesting ideas and interpretations
- immediate action, speech or commentary

Similarly, the ending of your composition or excerpt is very important. Try to introduce some suspense or surprise at the end; everyone likes to finish on a cliff-hanger!

●●● EXERCISE 3

Practise making brief planning notes by choosing one of the titles you discussed in Exercise 2 and then noting down how you might approach it. Think about:

- structure (plot if it is a story)
- setting
- narrative voice (1st or 3rd person)
- characters
- actions and events

●●● EXERCISE 4

Collect some of your favourite texts. These may include stories, autobiographies, magazine articles or diaries. For each one focus particularly on the opening paragraph.

How has each author begun their writing? What effect did their opening sentences have on you?

Discuss some of your favourite openings in class.

Language features

As mentioned in the introduction to this unit, there are several different genres that feature in the writing tasks, and every one has its own special language features that examiners may hope to find in the composition you write.

For example, if you choose to write a story, then you will be expected to include rich, descriptive language, making good use of adjectives, adverbs, similes and metaphors. It is also a good idea to incorporate some dialogue, using powerful verbs and adverbs (e.g. occasionally replacing the word 'said' with something more exciting!).

Similarly with an autobiographical account ('personal writing') you may be expected to show good use of time connectives to move the account along, or in a persuasive speech, to include rhetorical questions to get readers thinking, and some superlatives to emphasise your points.

Final word...

Writing creative compositions in examinations poses some difficult challenges for us all, and these include:

- interpreting questions and titles in exciting and unusual ways
- producing lively and colourful creative writing
- staying focused on your plan at all times
- working quickly in the time available

Very few novelists, biographers or speech writers like to feel so constrained by time limits, but even they have deadlines! The best way to prepare for this section of Paper 2 is to practise writing 'against the clock'. Once you have passed the examination, then you can spend months, even years, on a single story!

Discussion

The term 'descriptive writing' could be given to so many passages and texts. For the purposes of this unit (and the CE Writing Paper on which it is based) the term refers to a passage of writing in which descriptive language is used to describe a place, person or event.

Questions regularly appear in the writing section of the CE Paper in which you are invited to describe a particular place you have visited that may have left a lasting impression on you. Alternatively, you may be asked to write a short passage describing a person you know, a journey you have experienced, or an event that has taken place.

In all these options, you will be focusing on setting the scene and using descriptive language that appeals to the reader's senses, rather than narrating story action or producing dialogue.

As its name suggests, descriptive writing *describes* something to the reader. It is unlikely that the reader (or in this case the examiner) will have visited the place or person you are describing so your description will need to be detailed and interesting.

When descriptive writing is written well, it enables readers to imagine they are there, in the place that is featured, in the company of the person described or watching the event as it unfolds.

 Focus

IDEAS AND INTERPRETATIONS

- The parameters for some descriptive writing questions may be quite narrowly set; for example, describe a castle you have visited, or a favourite aunt or uncle you know. Others may be more open-ended and can be interpreted in various ways, for example, write a description of a place during a storm.
- Though the question may ask you to focus on a specific subject, in descriptive writing the creative ideas and interpretations may be evident in the way in which you describe it – the richness of your metaphors and similes, and the effects you are able to create through techniques such as personification and onomatopaiea (see 'Language features' on page 140).

MAKING NOTES

- Once you have decided on the subject for your piece of descriptive writing, it may be helpful to make some notes that will guide your writing and keep the ideas flowing once you get started. For example, if you are describing an old castle, some headings for your notes might include:
  - castle features
  - weather
  - sights, sounds and smells
  - landscape
  - local wildlife
  - ghostly tales and legends
- Remember that you are writing against the clock, so avoid making detailed notes that stretch over pages. A list of headings with just a few interesting words and phrases will be enough.

GETTING STARTED

- Once you have chosen your subject and made some planning notes to help you describe the different aspects of it, it is time to 'get started'. This can sometimes be where the trouble begins, and valuable time can be lost in trying to think of an opening sentence or two. A useful solution is to think of a camera lens. Imagine you have zoomed in on a tiny detail of your subject – a few pebbles on a beach, some wrinkles on a forehead, a cracked window pane on a house, or a clown's face at a circus. Describe these single features in detail, and then, gradually, widen your focus to take in (and describe) the whole scene.
- Always try to include some really interesting adjectives, adverbs and verbs in your opening sentences. If you can begin with a metaphor or simile, even better! The idea is to 'wow' your examiner with an opening line or two that shows off your writing talents and highlights your attention to detail.

●●● EXERCISE 3

Practise making planning notes for descriptive writing by jotting down some headings and key words or phrases that you might use for each of the following subjects:

- a deserted moor
- a disused chapel
- an elderly homeless person

●●● EXERCISE 4

Look around the classroom. Focus on one particular fitting or fixture – perhaps an old cabinet, a wall display or set of bookshelves.

Find a partner to work with. Face your chosen object and then ask your partner to face you (with their back to the object). You may tell him or her what the object is (this is not a guessing game), and then describe – in detail – the object you can see in front of you. Your partner may wish to ask you questions about the object, to ascertain more details about it.

LANGUAGE FEATURES

- As you might expect, the language used in writing of this kind is descriptive; each word needs to be carefully chosen to appeal to the reader's imagination and curiosity.
- Adjectives, adverbs and powerful verbs can all help to tell a story and paint a vivid scene in the reader's mind's eye.
- Try to include both literal and figurative (metaphorical) language. For example, a literal description like *the trees bent in the wind*, could be rewritten as *the great giants arched their backs against their enemy, the wind*.
- Introducing alliteration (e.g. *wild, whistling wind*) and onomatopaiea (*crash, whiz*) whilst thinking too about the rhythm of the language used can all increase its appeal.
- It is often a good idea to vary the length of your sentences, in order to create dramatic effect. Several long, complex sentences followed by one very short one, for example, can create a startling effect and keep readers alert and entertained.

 # Model Composition

QUESTION

Describe your favourite place of historic interest.

Here is one way to tackle this question. Naturally you will have different places that you may wish to describe. Read through the piece and then think about its structure and features, some of which have been highlighted with labels.

STUDLEY ROYAL GARDENS AND FOUNTAIN'S ABBEY, NORTH YORKSHIRE.

Lily pads gently congregate on emerald waters in a midsummer breeze. A pond skater pauses to take in the majestic views, before traversing the ripples that emanate from river banks, peppered with daisies. It is late afternoon at Studley Royal, and the guests are slowly dispersing.

> Begin by focusing on one specific detail or object, before widening the view.

Follies of white marble peer through their defences of mottled shade from high up on the valley sides, where the rooks call to one another and the intoxicating aroma of wild garlic fills the air.

> Use of metaphors for dramatic effect: 'peppered with daisies' and 'peer through their defences'.

Meandering along gravel paths, that frame neatly clipped lawns, the visitors join the last pilgrimage of the day to Fountain's Abbey. Past the ice-cream parlour, where the student waits, praying that the pages of his novel will last the distance between now and closing time. Another choc-ice would be greedy.

> Broadening the view to take in other land features and objects.

> Introducing characters and other viewpoints into the picture.

Through the trees, to the Deer Park beyond, flashes of brown and white dart across the copse. A fluffy tail here, a spotted brown back there, the elusive residents wait for the slow and steady trail of cars to wane, so they may prance in peace.

The leats lead on towards the Abbey. Framed in olive and sage greens, and carpeted in velvet grass, the great tower soars skywards, a monastic masterpiece and much-loved retreat.

The great arch stands firm, resisting centuries of Yorkshire wind and rain. Birds nest high above the visitors' heads, and watch for specks of white crumbs to appear on the green floor below.

Giant stones, where even greater columns once stood, now pose as seats for weary guests to perch a while, to fiddle with cameras and take tea from metal flasks. An errant little one braves a jump here and a climb there before being chided, in unison, by a warden and a red-faced parent. Grandparents chuckle.

Weather-beaten walls enclose a serene solitude. Though the monks are long gone, their legacy of peace and quiet contemplation endures. Members tiptoe, as they would in a library. Others gaze back from distant benches, forging indelible prints in their mind's eye, to be revisited in less tranquil moments back home.

> Use of alliteration: 'monastic masterpiece'.

> Reference to the 'historic interest' of the setting, as mentioned in the question.

leat: a manmade channel which supplies water to a watermill

❓ Writing Tasks (descriptive writing)

1 Write a detailed description of a lonely place which has made a strong impression on you.
2 Do you have any special possessions which are particularly important to you? Describe one of these in detail.
3 Write a piece of descriptive writing which begins with the following words: 'Beneath the dark and restless waves...'
4 Describe the atmosphere in a crowded airport lounge, the moment major flight delays are announced.
5 Produce a piece of descriptive writing entitled 'A Much-loved Pet'.
6 Write a description of a British seaside resort in winter.
7 Describe an event you have attended in which the weather spoiled proceedings.
8 Write a detailed description of a famous person whom you admire.

COMPOSITIONS

Discussion

A discursive text is a work of non-fiction which explores different views on a particular topic. It may highlight different responses to a controversial issue, exploring the reasons that lie behind the views shared.

Discursive writing makes the reader think. When we read about the views of others, in relation to a topic which we may know something about, inevitably we begin to consider our own position: do we agree or disagree with the views being put to us in the discursive text?

Discursive texts are, in some ways, like a conversation, in which the reader encounters the views of others on a shared topic of interest. Though the reader may not actually respond in words and phrases, like a real conversation, he or she will contribute by reflecting upon what is written down, and forming his or her own opinion in response. So, from the very beginning, the discursive writing needs to be interesting and thought-provoking to prompt a reaction from the reader.

Focus

IDEAS AND INTERPRETATIONS

- If there is a discursive writing question in the examination it is likely that it will be focused on a specific issue or topic, and so it will be less open to interpretation than a story or piece of descriptive prose. But there may still be scope for coming up with creative ideas, particularly in terms of how to begin (see 'Getting started' on the following page).
- The examiners will be looking to see if you have understood what the question is asking you to do: i.e. have you understood the issue, are you able to **see both sides**; can you step into someone else's shoes; can you understand – and articulate – another's viewpoint? It is important, then, that you read the question through several times so that you do not misinterpret it!

●●● EXERCISE 1

The topic of single-sex education – where boys and girls are taught separately – often invites opposing views. Can you think of some of the arguments for and against being taught in single-sex classrooms?

Discuss these arguments with a friend. Then think about how you might put these down in a discursive text.

●●● EXERCISE 2

What do you think about professional footballers' salaries? Are they paid too much? Or does the millions of pounds in ticket sales and the pleasure and enjoyment they give to many fans mean that they are worth every penny?

Whichever your viewpoint, try to see the argument from both sides. Write down a few points that summarise how people with different opinions from you might feel. Then practise articulating these views to a friend (you might want to begin by saying 'This is not what *I* think, but *some* people say...').

MAKING NOTES

- As stated earlier in this unit, there is little time in the examination for you to write your composition, let alone plan it sufficiently. So it may be inappropriate to devote several minutes to planning. For discursive essays, simply jot down some of the main arguments for and against the issue raised.
- You may be asked to share some of your own opinions in response to the given topic. If so, at the planning stage, write down a few phrases that sum up your feelings, which may be saved for the conclusion (or 'editorial' at the end).

GETTING STARTED

- A good way to begin a discursive essay is to write a sentence or two showing you understand that the issue in question is a controversial one and may be seen from several opposing viewpoints.
- Whatever the issue to be discussed, it is important to identify quickly what the opposing beliefs and opinions might be. It may be appropriate to begin with one extreme view: e.g. *For some, the idea of separating boys and girls for lessons seems antiquated and pointless...* This can then be matched against opposing views to set the discussion going.

LANGUAGE FEATURES

- To help you to switch between arguments, and give a commentary on the views held about a particular issue, several **connectives** and **phrases** can often be very useful: e.g. *on the other hand, however, on the contrary, some say, others believe.*
- Similarly, when switching between views, and looking at different arguments, it is important to use **new paragraphs** each time.
- The **passive tense** is also useful in presenting arguments and opinions in ways which can be distinguished from your own actual views: e.g. *it is said..., it is thought that...* or *such a view is widely held.*
- If you are invited to include your own opinions in response to a specific issue, then it will be necessary to include some first person commentary, preferably in the **conclusion** (or editorial): e.g. *I agree with the view that..., I do not believe that...* or *in my opinion...*

●●● EXERCISE 3

Practise identifying the main thrust of an argument by listening to a partner share his or her opinions about a particular issue. For example, ask a partner what he or she thinks about single-sex education (teaching boys and girls separately). Do they favour it, or do they think it is inappropriate? As they speak, make notes which sum up their thoughts in a series of bullet points.

●●● EXERCISE 4

How might you begin a discursive essay on the following issues or topics? Working in pairs or small discussion groups, consider the arguments for and against for at least one issue and then think of an interesting and provocative view to open your discursive essay.

- Vegetarianism
- Nuclear Power
- Wind farms
- Capital punishment

COMPOSITIONS

Model Composition

QUESTION

Why is fox-hunting such a controversial and emotive issue? What are the main arguments for and against this particular country pursuit?

Here is one way to tackle this challenging question. You may think of other arguments on both sides of the debate.

Look at the structure of the piece, the order it follows and the important features that have been highlighted.

> Introductory sentences to highlight different opinions – the source of debate.

The subject of fox-hunting has for many years been a source of great debate, and sometimes even hostility. People often feel very strongly about the issue – on both sides of the argument. Such debate is often portrayed as a battle of the classes, or seen as a conflict between countryside residents and city dwellers. But the topic gives rise to some important questions – about people's livelihoods and about alleged animal cruelty.

> Explain the subject of the essay. Set the scene by defining what fox-hunting is.

Hunting with hounds has now been outlawed in Britain, but for many years it prospered and hunts were a common sight across many parts of the countryside. In each hunt, a group of riders would follow a pack of hounds across fields in pursuit of a live fox. If the fox was caught, it was killed by the hounds.

> Introduce and explain views on one side of the argument.

There are some who believe that this is an effective form of pest control – perhaps even a fairer one, giving the fox a sporting chance of evading capture. Also, there are great numbers of people who depend upon fox-hunting for their livelihoods: those who breed and look after the hounds for each hunt, the horse trainers, the vets, even the blacksmiths. Some were concerned that if fox hunting was banned, people would actually lose their jobs, and horses and dogs may have to be put down because they no longer serve a useful function and the cost of running them could no longer be recouped by the hunt organisations. Similarly, there are those that believe that the fox population in rural areas is already too high, and banning fox hunting would make matters worse – with even more foxes attacking sheep, killing chickens and damaging crops.

> Switch to opposing views, with explanations.

However, others believe that the sport of fox-hunting is a barbaric practice which no longer belongs in a modern world. They say that hunting brings unnecessary and senseless cruelty upon the foxes, who, when caught, are ripped limb from limb by a pack of hungry dogs. Opponents of hunting suggest that there are far more humane ways of pest control – ways which are less costly, less time-consuming and more effective, like using poisons or guns.

Return to the question and reinforce answer, using same wording that appears in the question

The issue is an emotive one for the people on both sides of the argument. On the one hand, many of those who are in favour of fox hunting see any efforts to ban it as part of a campaign – led by city dwellers – to alter the customs and cultures of the countryside. Hunters believe that opponents do not understand the important role that fox-hunting plays in the life – and the preservation – of the countryside.

On the other hand, there are those for whom the idea of chasing after, and killing, a live fox is an abhorrent one. As a nation we love our animals and we often respond emotionally to any form of perceived animal cruelty, regardless of the purpose or circumstances.

Though the practice of hunting with hounds has been outlawed, there are many people around the country who are committed to seeing it legalised once again – and if the government changes, then who knows?

Interesting conclusion that suggests the debate is still continuing.

? Writing Tasks (discursive writing)

1   Is the term 'lawful killing' a contradiction? Can taking another person's life ever be right, even in wartime? Explore some of the issues and circumstances involved.

2   Discuss the different views held today on the subject of single-sex education. You may include some of your own opinions in the conclusion.

3   What are the views surrounding capital punishment today? If a murderer takes another person's life, do they deserve to keep their own? Highlight some of the issues on both sides of the argument.

4   Some professional football players can earn more in a week than many people earn in a year. Can this be right? Explore some of the opposing viewpoints on footballers' wages.

5   With the age of the World Wide Web truly upon us, does schooling need to take place in a single institution any more? Can children learn online from home? What are the arguments for and against traditional schooling?

6   For some people wind farms are the best option for a sustainable and environmentally-friendly future. For others, they are a blot on the landscape. Discuss some of the advantages and disadvantages of wind power.

7   Have you ever been unable to make a choice because none of your options appealed to you, or all of them did? Write a discursive text in which you introduce the decision you had to make and then explain the advantages and disadvantages of the options that were available to you at the time.

8   Religion can be a unifying force, bringing people together in shared values and beliefs; but it is also the biggest cause of wars across the world. Discuss how this contradiction can come about.

Discussion

In personal writing you may be sharing your likes and dislikes, recounting experiences you have had or articulating your opinion about something. In all circumstances, personal writing is just what it says: personal. It's about *you*.

This means, of course, that you cannot really 'get it wrong'. But you do need to express yourself in ways that are clear and interesting in order to gain good marks. Like the autobiographies you see in bookshops, personal writing is most effective when it offers readers an insight into the writer's thoughts and feelings in response to the experiences he or she has had.

Every Common Entrance examination will include one or two questions which ask for some form of personal writing – and these are very often tasks that ask you to focus upon a significant and memorable experience you may have had.

Why should the personal thoughts, emotions and memories of another be interesting for us to read about? Perhaps as humans we all sometimes need the reassurance that we are not alone, and that other people often share the same experiences and feel the same emotions from time to time. Personal writing can be comforting, amusing and, at times, inspiring...

... provided it is well written!

 ## Focus

IDEAS AND INTERPRETATIONS

- The question(s) that asks for personal writing in Section B of Paper 2 will usually prescribe quite closely what it is you should write about – usually a significant moment in your life when you learned an important lesson of some kind. So, with luck, if you choose to answer the question, it is because an event already springs to mind for you.
- Where the creative ideas and interpretations come in, is in how you recount your experience. The key is to be entertaining: embellish, exaggerate, enhance, enrich – just don't be dull! You will not be penalised for being creative with the truth, but you will lose marks for bland writing, so keep the recount exciting and colourful.

●●● EXERCISE 1

Working with a partner, take turns in describing your most embarrassing moment. If you cannot think of one, then recount a time when you felt frightened or lonely.

As you describe the experience, try to include details about how you felt at the time; this usually helps listeners (and readers) to empathise with you, and enjoy the episode more.

●●● EXERCISE 2

Think about a time when you had to face something you were dreading – perhaps some examinations, a trip to the dentist, or a solo in a concert.

Can you remember how you felt as the ordeal approached? Write down some words and phrases that help to exaggerate your feelings at the time. You could include some metaphors and similes for effect, like 'my stomach was doing somersaults' or 'I felt like I was walking to the gallows'.

MAKING NOTES

- It may be helpful to jot down one or two key words and phrases that will jog your recollection of your experiences as you write about them: key moments, feelings felt, things that were said, and so on.
- Some personal writing questions ask for your predictions or preferences rather than your memories, in which case, you may wish to note down what they are, with several different reasons: e.g. a celebrity you would most like to meet and why.

GETTING STARTED

- Read the question several times to ensure that you have the measure of it. Valuable marks can be lost by misinterpreting what you are being asked to do and then recounting the wrong sort of event!
- As with most forms of composition, it is a good idea to 'get straight into the action' which, in this case, means getting into your thoughts and feelings quickly – rather than spending too much time setting the scene. You could begin with a bold statement, like, *For me, there can be no greater sportsman than Sir Steve Redgrave...*

LANGUAGE FEATURES

- Some personal writing – particularly recounts of experiences and events – will be **chronological** in form, and will require **time connectives** like *first of all, later, finally, meanwhile*.
- Your own personal thoughts and feelings are very important in this form of writing and so inevitably you will be using the **first person narrative** (*I* believe, *I* found *my* seat).
- **Adjectives** and **adverbs** that help to set the scene and build a vivid picture of an experience for readers (who were not there with you) are very useful indeed. Keep your writing sharp and colourful. Try to remember that readers need to know how things looked, sounded, smelt and felt.
- **Similes** and **metaphors** are very useful ways of building tension and creating dramatic effect, by exaggerating and emphasising your feelings. So, for example, rather than saying *It was nearly time for the exam*, you might say *The hand of fate was beckoning me into the cold cell-like room, where the empty tables were waiting, in cemetery rows*.

●●● EXERCISE 3

Practise making notes by thinking about who your favourite sports personality is. Write down their name, what they do, and then, using bullet points and key words or phrases, write down some reasons to explain why you rate this person so highly.

These notes could be turned into a piece of personal writing by expanding on each point, giving examples to illustrate each one and then sharing your thoughts and feelings.

●●● EXERCISE 4

How might you begin a piece of personal writing for each of the following titles? Work with a partner and jot down some possible opening lines for each one.

a) A concert to remember!
b) My favourite cuisine
c) Nightmare holiday
d) The greatest singer
e) A lonely experience

●●● EXERCISE 5

Practise using adjectives to set the scene by writing down some descriptive words and phrases for each of the following settings for personal writing:

a) An exam room
b) A nativity play
c) A church christening
d) A school disco
e) A campsite in the rain

COMPOSITIONS

Model Composition

QUESTION

Write about a time when you felt acutely embarrassed.

Here is one response to this question. You will have your own incidents that come to mind. Look at the structure of the piece, the order it follows and the important features that have been highlighted.

> Straight into the action – set the scene in a quick, punchy sentence or two.

It was the annual school disco. I remember the heady cocktail of aftershave, perfume and Cherryade that wafted down the corridors as I arrived, suited and booted for a good night out, aged 12.

The music thumped and throbbed. The red and orange lights flashed like traffic cones. DJ Derek spat indecipherable words into a microphone and lots of girls screamed in excitement.

> Interesting adjectives and similes to help build a picture for the reader.

> Give some background to the story to build tension and increase reader's amusement.

Daily life for me usually consisted of battling with my two brothers, playing mini-rugby and attending a school for boys. Girls rarely entered my world – sadly. I remember turning a tomato colour if a girl even looked in my direction. Should a young lady be foolish enough to speak to me, she would usually be entertained (or put off) by a strange performance of stuttering, shuffling and continuous apologising, until I could escape.

Tonight, then, was what they call a 'big night'. Flanked by my two best friends, Patrick and Jonathan, I bopped and boogied, wriggled and writhed to the sound of Ghostbusters. The girls danced on one side of the hall, we danced on the other – and the teachers stood, like prison wardens, betwixt us, with frowns that said: 'One move, mister, and it's solitary confinement for you.'

> Another simile (prison wardens) for comic effect.

> Powerful verbs to add drama: *thumped* and *sauntered*.

I remember, as if it were yesterday, the moment Michelle walked into the crowded room. '99 Red Balloons' had just started. As the bass line thumped out its catchy rhythm, Michelle and her mermaids sauntered across the dance floor and took up their positions near the stage, where the coloured bulbs played games with their hair.

She was a goddess: there was no other word. Had I the courage of a decorated war veteran I might – just might – have talked to her. But, as it was, my role was to be the adoring fan from afar. Now she was in the room, my dancing seemed even more ridiculous than it had been before. In a fit of self-consciousness I quit my losses and moved, as casually as I could, towards the 'bar' and asked the 'bartender' for another Cherryade (on the rocks).

> Use of exaggeration in a short sentence for extra effect: 'She was a goddess'.

Then it happened. Through the crowds of sweaty bodies, Michelle's friends came looking.

For me.

I still remember their sweet-sounding words, that rolled off their tongues and into my soul, where they still rest today:

'Michelle wants to see you – outside.'

The initial shock had, of course, left me speechless. But, slowly the fog lifted and I was able to splutter out something that resembled 'okay'.

Strutting like John Travolta I began my syncopated steps back across the dance floor and out through the doors, into the playground below.

There she was. Seated on the bench, in the 'quiet area'. My heart was a fireworks display. As casual as one could be at the feet of a living idol I strolled towards her. She stared at me, her eyes wide open, probably in adoration.

'NO! Not him!' she said. 'I meant his friend... the tall one.'

> Useful metaphor: 'my heart was a fireworks display'.

> The embarrassment (and tragedy) is revealed in the final punch line.

? Writing Tasks (personal writing)

1 Write about a time when you were punished for something that you did not do. How did you feel?
2 What is your favourite sport, and why?
3 Write about the happiest moment in your life to date.
4 Describe a time when you felt anxious about something and then, once it was all over, you wondered what all the fuss was about.
5 Write about a time when a parent or guardian embarrassed you in public.
6 If you could be an animal, what would you be, and why?
7 Describe a person (living or deceased) whom you greatly admire. Explain why he or she inspires you.
8 Imagine you are setting off on a long journey into space. You are allowed just two luxuries. What will you take with you, and why?

Discussion

Though there are many forms of persuasive texts – from advertising slogans to holiday brochures – for the purposes of a Common Entrance paper, persuasive writing often means a speech of some sort. It can also be a letter or an article. You may be offered a 'motion' – a statement to be debated – and then asked to produce a speech proposing or opposing it.

Persuasive writing should do what it says: *persuade* listeners, or readers, to act in some way, whether it means voting, joining or giving money, and so on. Most writing genres will have some intended impact on readers, but persuasive writing, perhaps, can have the most measurable effect of all, if written well.

From Prime Ministers to church leaders, military commanders to head teachers, many people in authority rely on the power of their speeches to influence the opinions of others and ultimately change hearts and minds.

 ## Focus

IDEAS AND INTERPRETATIONS

- Usually the subject of the speech will be given for you in the question, and this may take the form of an actual debate motion (beginning *This House believes...*) or a sentence or two explaining the issue you need to write about. If you are given a choice of writing either **for** or **against** a particular statement, then try not to spend too much time deciding! It really does not matter which side you are on – you can still write a good speech!
- It is often a good idea to include some personal experiences or other anecdotes (true stories) in your speech. This may help to strengthen your argument and increase the impact you have on your audience.

● ● ● EXERCISE 1

Have you ever been persuaded by another person's speech? Have you ever participated in a debate?

Share your experiences of listening to and writing speeches with a partner. Why do you think some speeches are more persuasive than others?

● ● ● EXERCISE 2

Do you know why most debate motions traditionally begin with the words 'This House believes...'?

See if you can find out more information on the origins of this famous phrase, and then share your findings in class.

MAKING NOTES

- Most good speeches will have several distinct points or arguments to them, and these need to be recorded first of all as bullet points. Once you have decided whether your speech will be for or against a particular motion, then you can set about thinking up persuasive arguments to back up your point of view.
- For each argument you make, it is a good idea to include some evidence. This may come in the form of anecdotes, examples, quotations and data. If you do not have any real evidence in mind, then use your imagination!

GETTING STARTED

- It is usually a good idea to begin a persuasive speech with confirmation of which side of the debate you are on, i.e. *I am in favour of a curfew for children for the following reasons...*
- Then progress through your points, explaining each one in detail and, if possible, supporting them with evidence of some kind. Use a separate paragraph for each argument you make.

LANGUAGE FEATURES

- Questions are a useful way of inviting a listener to consider an issue and form an opinion. **Rhetorical questions** (ones for which there really can only be one answer) are a particularly useful tool when seeking to influence someone's thinking: e.g. *Do you really want to live in a place where children are imprisoned in their own homes?* (Of course not!).
- Similarly, **superlatives** can help to create an impact on listeners – the greatest, the best, the worst, the happiest, and so on. Such claims may be exaggerations, but they serve a purpose, helping to convince readers to share your viewpoint.
- Most speeches contain words and phrases that help to argue your case by showing **cause** and **effect**: e.g. *consequently, therefore, this means that, inevitably.*
- **Emotional language** is often used too: powerful adjectives and verbs, strong similes and metaphors, and abstract nouns to show feelings. Such language can appeal to readers' or listeners' hearts rather than their heads!

●●● EXERCISE 3

Imagine you have been asked to write a speech either for or against the following motion:

> *This House believes that children under 16 should not be allowed outside unaccompanied after dark.*

Practise note-making by jotting down some separate arguments for or against this statement. You might want to consider: safety issues, freedom, crime and disorder, parental control, behaving responsibly, health and fitness, socialising with others and playing too many computer games!

●●● EXERCISE 4

Look back at the notes you made for Exercise 3. See if you can put them in order, beginning with the most convincing argument.

Share your views with a partner. Practise opening your arguments with a convincing sentence or two. Then make similar notes for the opposing side. Can you counter the original arguments that you made?

COMPOSITIONS

Model Composition

QUESTION

Write a debate speech either for or against the following motion:

'This House believes that books are better entertainment than television.'

Read the following speech, in favour of the motion. Take note of its structure and language features, highlighted here with labels.

Introductory sentence to indicate whether you are arguing for or against the motion.

Powerful adjectives, similes and metaphors for impact.

Bold sentence to open your argument, supported by explanation and provocative questions.

Effective use of humorous anecdotes to appeal to readers.

Supporting example, which may be common to many readers.

I believe that books provide a better source of entertainment than television.

Books are good for the brain. They stimulate the imagination, projecting images into our heads, keeping our minds healthy and happy. What does television do for our imagination? Most of us watch television programmes like robots, passively receiving the images, sounds and meanings that are pumped into our minds without question or comment.

Through books we may enjoy stories, plays and poems at our own pace. We may ponder characters, make predictions and imagine scenarios at our leisure. We are not rushed. Yet when we watch television, we are denied the time we need to consider, reflect and learn. Our eyes and ears are assaulted by a battery of mediocre material, packed into TV schedules like sausage meat.

There are no advertisements in books. There is nothing worse than watching a piece of drama or following a documentary only to be rudely interrupted by an insipid man in rubber gloves telling you how to get the grease off your cooker, or a lady informing you that her constipation cleared up within minutes of taking some magic pill. With books you can suspend your disbelief without fear that someone will burst your bubble any minute. Fantasy worlds can seem real; characters can come to life.

When you read a book the fictional characters you encounter are your own to keep. You interpret the descriptions in a unique way, and though several of your friends may claim to have read the same story, and know the characters as well as you do, the images they have in their minds will be different from yours, because we all imagine faces and features in different ways. How many of us have been disappointed by the Harry Potter movies because we were expecting to see the characters that formed in our heads when we read the books?

And what about the expense? How many books can you buy for the price of a new television? How many more can you keep purchasing for the cost of the licence fee and the electricity to run it? If there was a power cut, the 'telly addicts' would be left staring at the wall with vacant faces and empty heads. With books all you need is a candle to read by.

There is a comfort to be found at the end of a busy day, in picking up a favourite storybook and escaping into one's own fantasy world, where fictional friends await you. The act of reading words on a page is soothing. Surely there can be no better form of entertainment.

> More questions to make readers stop and think.

> Rounding off the speech with an appealing image and closing statement.

? Writing Tasks (persuasive writing)

1   Write a speech for **or** against the re-introduction of corporal punishment in schools (smacking and using the cane).

2   Imagine you have met a person who has no interest in computers at all, and refuses to buy one. Write a short speech persuading this person to see the advantages of having a computer.

3   Write a debate speech **either** proposing **or** opposing the following motion: *This House believes that all British police should be armed.*

4   Some people believe that the British monarchy no longer has a purpose in our modern society and we should become a republic with a democratically elected president. Do you agree? Write a speech either for or against keeping the monarchy.

5   Write a debate speech for **or** against the following motion: *This House believes that in this overpopulated world, new parents should be allowed to have two children only.*

6   Imagine you are a newly appointed head teacher of your school. You are about to attend your first governors' meeting, at which you will be expected to make a short speech setting out your ambitious plans for the school. Write this speech.

7   Write a debate speech **either** proposing **or** opposing the following motion: *This House believes that new technology combined with modern life styles mean that children should no longer be herded together into school cattle sheds. Pupils should be taught online from home.*

8   Imagine that the elections for Form Captain are approaching. Write a speech explaining why people should vote for you.

COMPOSITIONS

5.5 Narrative Writing

💬 Discussion

The word 'narrative' refers to a collection of different events woven together in the form of a story. For the purposes of the Common Entrance writing paper, it means 'storywriting'.

Whole stories take time to write, but you can score high marks in the exam by writing a really exciting excerpt or chapter from an imaginary story. Why not try to produce one of the following narratives:

- A lively story opening, with some exciting action or dialogue
- An excerpt from the middle of a story, where something dramatic happens
- Several short excerpts from the same story, to show the passage of time
- A flashback or commentary, where a character shares his or her thoughts about something that has happened to them

In all of the above examples, the story is, of course, an imaginary one, and it may not even be complete, but the excerpts will give you a chance to show off your narrative writing skills. For each one, think carefully about how you will begin, what action takes place, and how you will finish the excerpt.

All stories – even the greatest ones of all – have moments when the pace slows as the writer concentrates on building contexts, introducing characters and explaining scenarios. Then there may be other times when readers are gripped. The task in a writing exam is to produce the latter: a short piece of enthralling story narration that gets straight to the heart of the action!

> ### ●●●● EXERCISE 1
>
> Think of some of your favourite stories. Obtain copies of each one and then try to find a really exciting page or two in each. It may be a thrilling moment of drama, conflict or suspense – a scene which had you enthralled when you first read it.
>
> In each case, consider how the author creates such a gripping read. Think about:
>
> - descriptive language
> - interesting characters
> - lively dialogue
> - significant events or crises that occur
> - exciting cliff-hangers at the end of a page or chapter

Focus

IDEAS AND INTERPRETATIONS

- Very often questions on narrative writing will offer a title to be interpreted in some way, or a sentence or two to be included in a story. Try to use your imagination to come up with some interesting ideas if you can, but do not spend too much time planning your ideas: you need to get writing quickly!

- Focus carefully on the words in the title or sentence that is given to you in the question. With luck some ideas will come to you, which you can then develop as you go along. You don't have to think of an entire story plot! Just get straight into the action and try to keep the reader interested.

- Once you have thought of a story idea, based on the title you have been given, think about the following things:
  - *where* your story takes place
  - *who* is in your story
  - *what* happens
  - *why* readers will find it exciting to read

MAKING NOTES

- As with any storywriting, planning is important, although since you will be writing against the clock, the notes need to be brief. Use bullet points, or a diagram – like a mind-map or spidergram – to record your ideas. Use these words from the previous section to guide your thinking: *where, who, what* and *why*.

- Keep your planning notes brief and to the point. Your plan is a working document for you, so use it as a way of keeping your thoughts and ideas focused. If you think you may run out of time in the writing exam, then refer to your plan and write a few sentences to show the examiner what would happen next in the story.

GETTING STARTED

- Beginning a story is rather like entering a cold swimming pool: just plunge in and get writing. Hovering about on the edge, worrying too much about your opening sentence will waste valuable time and spoil your creative mood. It is true that how you begin is important – an exciting piece of dialogue or action-packed narration usually works well – but often creative ideas will only reveal themselves once you start putting pen to paper.

- Remember, of course, to write in paragraphs from the beginning. Valuable marks may be lost when examiners face great blocks of unbroken scrawl to mark.

●●● EXERCISE 2

Practise thinking of some story ideas quickly and efficiently using the following titles as a starting point:

- Trapped
- The Day That Changed My Life
- Mistaken Identity
- Summer Voyage

●●● EXERCISE 3

Look again at the sample story titles in Exercise 2. Then practise making story plans for each one, remembering to include:

- a brief outline of the plot or scene you will be writing about
- character summaries
- details about the setting
- any significant events planned

●●● EXERCISE 4

See if you can write the first two sentences for each of the following story titles:

- The Steep Climb
- Evacuated
- Time Out
- Guilty as Charged

LANGUAGE FEATURES

- In narrative writing **time connectives** are useful tools to move the story along and connect those events that were referred to in the definition at the beginning of this section: e.g. *later*, *meanwhile*, *suddenly*, *finally*.

- Just like descriptive writing, narrative writing requires interesting **adjectives**, **verbs** and **adverbs** to engage readers' interest and make them want to read on. Similarly, try to include some fresh and exciting **similes** and **metaphors** as you narrate the action, to create dramatic effect.

- Bring characters to life by allowing them to respond to the events that are unfolding around them. None of us are robots. We all express **feelings** in response to what happens around us, whether it be anger, fear, pride, or love, and fictional characters need to do the same.

- **Dialogue** is also important, especially when seeking to display your storywriting skills, so remember to include some exciting speech, narrated through powerful verbs and adverbs (i.e. interesting synonyms for 'said'!).

> ### ● ● ● EXERCISE 5
>
> Working in pairs, see how many interesting descriptive phrases you can come up with to describe the following story settings. Focus especially on powerful adjectives, abstract nouns, similes and metaphors.
>
> - A sandy beach
> - A rainforest
> - A lift
> - Mount Everest

 # Model Composition

QUESTION

Begin a story with the following line:

'Within seconds I knew that I had made the wrong decision...'

Below is one interpretation of this question; you will have your own ideas. Read through the script and take note of the different language features, highlighted with labels.

Begin with the exact wording in the question.	*Within seconds I knew that I had made the wrong decision. The ruts either side of the Land Rover swelled to trench-sized gulleys, awash with red, muddy water. The rain beat a rhythm against the cracked windscreen. The wheels lost their traction and slowly sank into the quagmire. We were stuck.*	
	'I said we should have taken the other path, but you wouldn't –'	Continue with clues as to what the decision had entailed and why it was the wrong one.
	'Alright!' I snapped.	
	'Well,' continued Niall, high on the satisfaction of being right, 'I thought this one would lead to a dead end. You just get a feeling for these things when you've been out here as long as I have.'	

Some background to develop the characters.

Niall had indeed been in Kenya for an eternity. And I had visited him every year since those early days. Three years my junior, he had always been the brave one of the family – the one that refused to conform; the one for whom a smart suit and an office job had always seemed like a prison sentence.

And now here we were, together again: two young bucks taking on the world.

And getting stuck. My air-conditioned office in Canary Wharf seemed light years away now.

'So what do we do now?' I said defeatedly. 'It's obvious we can't get any further along. But we can't turn round either.'

'Fear not intrepid brother of mine. For I have friends in high places... literally.' Niall grinned. His cheerful face, bronzed by so many African summers, cracked into a mischievous grin, revealing pearly white teeth.

Include lively dialogue to maintain readers' interest.

'Okay. So you know someone who can get us out?' I asked.

'Certainly do, bruv'. And he's that-a-way.' Niall pointed to the mountain village behind us. 'He's got a winch too. He can tow us out.'

As we opened the doors of the vehicle, the god of rain chose that precise moment to give us everything he had. It came down in torrents: millions of giant-sized silver globules, each one capable of soaking you to the bone.

Use of metaphors for dramatic effect.

Slowly we trudged on, back up the track, towards the crossroads. My new boots, bought especially for this most recent African adventure, now resembled soggy chamois leathers. My Indiana Jones hat was nothing but a sponge on my head. But our spirits remained high, buoyed up by my brother's incessant singing.

Until he fell.

Very short paragraph of three words – to cause maximum impact.

I hadn't even realised he'd gone down at first. The sound of rain lashing against my ears had almost deafened me. But eventually I realised the singing had stopped. I turned around, expecting to see Niall's sopping wet face behind me, but saw nothing. Then, glancing further down the track, I saw him lying there, face down in the mud.

Try to end on a 'cliff-hanger' if you can.

And he wasn't moving.

COMPOSITIONS

❓ Writing Tasks (narrative writing)

1. Write a story beginning with the following line: 'As I sat there and waited for my turn, the palms of my hands began to sweat and my throat soon felt dry...'

2. Write a story that contains the following line: 'It wasn't me!'

3. Compose a story of your own which begins: 'No one could ever have known where the road would lead us...'

4. Produce a piece of narrative writing on one of the following themes:
   - Friendship
   - Making sacrifices
   - Secrets

5. Write a story that contains the words 'Action stations!'

6. Narrate an original story on the theme of love.

7. Begin writing a story with the following words: 'Ready, aim, fire...'

8. Write a story which includes the following line: 'At this altitude, collapsing was not a faint possibility, it was a likelihood.'